LIFE IS BEAUTIFUL

PRAISE FOR *LIFE IS BEAUTIFUL*

"In *Life Is Beautiful* Jim Cusumano takes us on a practical journey of heart and spirit. With his scientific background coupled with his ability to illuminate the wisdom of the greatest spiritual traditions, Dr. Cusumano eloquently bridges the worlds of science and mysticism, bringing clarity to both. His stories of the amazing people he's known and the remarkable things he's done make for a thrilling read as well as a deep learning experience."

—Gay Hendricks, PhD
Best-selling author of *The Big Leap* and *Conscious Loving Ever After*

"*Life is Beautiful* is an essential sourcebook for humanity to manifest at our collective potential—spiritual, social and scientific. It has brought together with great clarity, wisdom of the ages, spiritual physics with cutting-edge quantum physics and the very latest understanding of Consciousness itself. It is a book of epic importance, vital for our culture now. I have reread it several times. It can illuminate all of our teachings and can serve us to manifest our **HIGHEST** purposes in life."

—Barbara Marx Hubbard
President, The Foundation For Conscious Evolution

"In *Life is Beautiful*, Jim Cusumano, in his typical style, beautifully balanced between the pragmatic and the spiritual, brings the most important questions in life into clear focus, and provides easily implementable ways to answer them—and live them. Read it and reap—your life will be beautiful."

—Lance Secretan, PhD
Author of *ONE* and *Inspire*, Former CEO of Manpower, Inc.

"*Life is Beautiful* is a transformational book that will allow you to inherit your connection to spirit … and to live a limitless life more powerfully, lovingly and with more happiness! Bravo!"

—**Kathy Gardarian**
CEO Qualis International, Inc.

"Jim Cusumano's book *Life is Beautiful* is wonderfully clear, life-affirming advice from a deeply experienced spiritually-grounded global business leader."

—**Hazel Henderson**
Author of *Mapping the Global Transition to the Solar Age*
President, Ethical Markets Media (USA and Brazil)

"In *Life Is Beautiful*, Jim Cusumano raises almost all the questions that matter—questions that matter for your life and the life of others around you; that matter for now in the context of what you do today and the next day, and for what you do with the rest of your life. The conclusions he reaches regard the nature and import of consciousness, and they closely parallel the conclusions I have myself reached in the span of the last several decades. They are phrased simply, and simply beautifully. I recommend this book to everyone who is interested in life's big questions, which are also the "little" but vital questions of everyday existence."

—**Ervin Laszlo, PhD**
Founder and President of The Club of Budapest
Director and Co-founder of the Ervin Laszlo
Institute for Advanced Study

"This incredible *magnum opus* Jim Cusumano has produced, *Life is Beautiful: 12 Rules*, could more accurately have been entitled *Jim's All Inclusive Theory of Everything*. This really is a capstone book coming on the heels of his two earlier books each of which served, in its way, as a stepping stone for what Jim brilliantly and humbly serves up here. This heartfelt reflection goes way beyond his earlier book on work-life balance to something that effectively weaves into a tapestry of his observations from being stunningly successful in business, entertainment, science, quantum physics and Vedic theory. Every single literate person on the planet would be well served to immerse themselves in Jim's poignantly deep, and deftly spun, articulation of how the universe works, and how we can most effectively work with it to achieve everything we'd like to manifest. This is the first work I know of that so eloquently and powerfully describes the science and art behind all of this which he calls "Spiritual Physics." Go no further if you want to really understand who we are as individuals in the cosmos, how we interact with each other and the various planes of reality, and how all of that is a spiritual journey we can take with whatever degree of skill and joy that we choose. Life truly is beautiful precisely because he gives us the tools to choose for it to be so, and provides us with all the insights we require in a single volume to make it so. It has worked magnificently for Jim, and it will for you as well."

—Rinaldo S. Brutoco
Founding President and CEO, World Business Academy

"This is a book that wakes you up! With discipline and grace, Dr. Cusumano brings the voice of maturity and wisdom to life's most important and most challenging questions. Seamlessly integrating science, spirituality and psychology, he provides the reader with an easy to understand, clearly languaged roadmap for the journey to our greatest potential and our most essential selves. *Life is Beautiful's* universal message around power of purpose touches the pulse of all our lives."

—David Surrenda, PhD
Founder and Dean, John F. Kennedy University
Graduate School of Holistic Studies
Co-author of ***Retooling on the Run: Real Change for Leaders with No Time***

LIFE IS BEAUTIFUL

12 Universal Rules

JAMES A. CUSUMANO, PhD

Waterfront Press

Published by Waterfront Press
www.waterfrontdigitalpress.com

For Inez,
Doreen, Polly and Julia

BOOKS BY
JAMES A. CUSUMANO

Freedom from Mid-East Oil
(coauthors: Jerry B. Brown and Rinaldo S. Brutoco)

Cosmic Consciousness
A Journey to Well-being, Happiness and Success

Balance: The Business-Life Connection

CONTENTS

ACKNOWLEDGEMENTS

Writing a book is never a solo journey. And it is not an easy task to list all those responsible for contributing in some way to the conception, structure, writing and completion of a book. I won't even try to be comprehensive as the list is a long one, and I trust that all those involved and not mentioned here, know that I carry them with gratitude in my heart and soul.

I want to recognize that this path of discovery has been facilitated by my study of the detailed works of a number of wise sages who expressed their insights over the millennia, as well as through numerous discussions with many of the "giants" in my life—people who have inspired me toward my Life Purpose.

From times past, I have drawn on the wisdom of Buddha, Patanjali, Rumi, Dalai Lama Gendun Drup, Krishna, Mohammad, Confucius, Lao-Tzu, Jesus and many more avatars. In current times, significant among my teachers have been Michael Bernard Beckwith, Paulo Coelho, Neville Goddard, Jean Houston, David Steindl-Rast, Eckhart Tolle, Ken Wilbur, Marianne Williamson, and most particularly, my good friend Deepak Chopra. Deepak especially has often clarified and nurtured my thinking on many of the issues and concepts I encountered.

I am deeply grateful for the many stimulating and enlightening discussions over the last 40 years with my dear friend and long-time business partner, Ricardo Levy. By teaching a course in entrepreneurship at Stanford University and through his publications, Ricardo has made substantial contributions to understanding the *Meaning of Life* and how to live a life of personal and professional fulfillment[1]

The contributions of a few individuals were so significant that the end result would never have happened without them. In this respect, I first and foremost honor the spirit of my mother and father, Carmela and Charles Cusumano. They challenged me from day one to reach for the stars, and not only supported my questioning the *status quo*, but saw it as my path to a better understanding of life.

There are several close friends—highly conscious intellectual "giants," whose perspectives, insights and arguments over the years, provided me with the deeper understanding of humanity and the universe that inspired me to write this book. In alphabetical order, they are Madeleine Austin, Bob Baran, Michel Boudart, Rinaldo Brutoco, Tommy Davis, Richard Fleming, Kathy Gardarian, Gay Hendricks, Diane Ladd, Ervin Laszlo, Manfred J. D. Low, Lance Secretan, John H. Sinfelt and David Surrenda. While I was the instrument of authorship for the concepts and ideas presented here, any truly incisive insight surely emanated from my discussions with these "giants."

I continue to appreciate the patience and incisive suggestions of my literary agent, William Gladstone. And I treasure the questions and comments from my three daughters, Doreen, Polly and Julia. Nine-year-old Julia should be especially recognized, as she showed little mercy with her deep and honest questions, comments and critiques! They, of course, helped me gain a better understanding of myself and life in general

As to the unwavering support and consolation that every author seeks and needs during those dark hours of the creative process, there is but one person I hold in special regard, and that's my loving wife, Inez. Her critique of early drafts added substantially to the readability and accessibility of the book's content. None of my writings would have ever seen the light of day without her insight, support and understanding.

To these very special individuals and to those not mentioned here, all of whom have nourished my spirit along my life path, I send my sincerest thanks and a heartfelt Namaste.

"Know thyself!" [1,2]

---

1 *Gnothi Seauton ("Know Thyself")* is inscribed above the entrance to the temple of Apollo at Delphi, site of the revered and sacred Oracle. This is arguably the most profound and valuable advice ever exhorted upon humanity.

2 Quotes without a reference are those by the author.

PREFACE

This is a book about a big question.

Sooner or later, most of us come face to face with this question—*What is the meaning of life*, and its direct corollary—*How can I live a happy life?* Why do some people seem to sail through their life journey with a smile and positive attitude? And most of what they seek seems to eventually come their way.

The reason is that they have either consciously or unconsciously discovered underlying, fundamental universal truths. And in following the path created for them by these truths or rules, they cannot help but do well. In fact, I hope to convince you that doing well is the natural intended outcome for all species in this universe.

The fact is, *life is beautiful,* and it truly does take more effort to live a miserable one than a beautiful one!

This is something we might think about as we approach the sunset years of our life. Then, it can become a perennial quest to find answers to life's "big questions." I believe the reason for this is that in time we begin to quiet the noise in our intensely connected modern world and finally hear some things that were always there in each and every one of us. For instance, "What am I doing with my life? Does it really matter? Where am I going? Will I have made a difference when I'm gone?"

Wouldn't it be great to find the answers to these questions, sooner rather than later? It would certainly make for a happier, more fulfilling life.

The answers can come sooner than you think. You don't have to wait for retirement, or worse, until that moment when you are about to shed your body. The answers can be rewarding and inspiring beyond all expectations. Furthermore, they can set you on a trajectory towards long-term fulfillment.

My experiences based on a circuitous life journey to answer these questions, and my enthusiasm to share what I've learned, have been the driving force for creating this monograph. My sole professional purpose and passion at this point in my life is to communicate what I have learned in the hope that I can make a positive difference in the lives of others, and show that *Life Is Beautiful.*

My Path

My path has not been an easy one. I made lots of mistakes along the way. But it was a magnificent learning experience and continues to be so. In retrospect, I would do it all over again!

My career followed a path over several decades through the fields of entertainment and science. It began for me as a teenager, when I found success in the U.S. as a recording artist. Years later, after a PhD in physical chemistry, I subsequently and progressively moved first to my role as a research scientist and then as an executive in corporate America; next, to co-founder and CEO of two public Silicon Valley technology companies; followed by executive producer of an internationally-distributed feature film; and now, serving as owner of an award-winning five-star holistic castle hotel and spa in the Czech Republic. The details of my journey can be found elsewhere.[3,4]

As I navigated these five eclectic professional lives with increasing levels of insight and what many consider success, I formulated 12 Universal Rules. I uncovered them as I studied the lives of numerous deeply enlightened individuals, and measured these rules against what worked and didn't work in my own life. I eventually realized that life does not have to be extensively complicated or painful, and the answers to many of those profound questions that challenge us at one time or another, have already been answered long ago by wise thinkers and significant change-makers.

Perhaps more important, as well as keenly pragmatic is that by understanding the answers to these questions, I discovered a set of guidelines that enabled me to live an increasingly "successful" and fulfilling life. The essence of my discoveries is what I want to share in the hope that it will resonate and provide tools and guidance to answers that feel right for you. The end result you will find is to create a *life that is beautiful.*

Physics Meets Philosophy

Over the years, I have been increasingly drawn to the teachings of Eastern philosophers. Because of my training in the physical sciences, this fascination intensified as I began to discover the parallels between Eastern thought and the findings of modern quantum physics. I was amazed that wise thinkers, who lived thousands of years ago, could even remotely approach the same conclusions that highly-educated, talented, modern day physicists could "see" only though the eyes of complex mathematics and the deepest concepts of theoretical physics.

So profound are these findings that most professional physicists prefer to ignore them because they penetrate the sphere of metaphysics and are not considered "appropriate" areas of study for a well-educated scientist whose professional life is firmly grounded in the tenets of the scientific method. I personally have not felt this way, in fact, quite the contrary. This is not a courageous position on my part. Perhaps, it's because my current professional pursuits no longer fall directly in the scientific arena, and my livelihood and security don't depend upon my being in lockstep agreement with the majority of the global scientific community.

The Query

Over the years, through my study of the parallels between ancient Eastern thought and modern physics, and guided by findings of several current-day wise thinkers, I have come to conclusions I find helpful in leading me along my life path. Specifically, I am referring to practical answers to important timeless questions that many of us sooner or later struggle with, including: *Where did I come from? Why am I here? What is my true Life Purpose? How can I live my Life Purpose to maximum personal and professional fulfillment? Is there a non-physical part of me and if so, what will happen to it when I die?*

All of these age-old questions relate directly to one fundamental inquiry: *What is the meaning of life?* The answer to this question will enable you to see that *Life is Beautiful* and with a little effort you can live your life in total fulfillment.

Some of my initial thoughts and conclusions found their way into my last two books, *COSMIC CONSCIOUSNSS: A Journey to Well-being, Happiness and Success*[5] and *BALANCE: The Business-Life Connection.*[6] There I discuss how I discovered direct correlations connecting *Life Purpose* and long-term personal and professional *Fulfillment*. I have drawn on some of these conclusions here and extended them as intimate components of the 12 Universal Rules.

This has had a major impact on what I and many others perceive as personal and professional success and the means to long-term happiness. I see an inextricable link between personal and professional values on one hand, and long-term happiness on the other. Even more fundamental and firmly entrenched underneath these values is a universal purpose that is embraced by all consciousness-aware species. I will share with you my thoughts concerning this purpose. My hope is that this will stimulate and clarify your own thinking on these important issues. In truth, I believe they are the only ones that truly matter.

Means to The End

This book is divided into two parts. In *Part I, The Reason for Your Existence: 12 Universal Rules of Life.* Here I provide insights and principles that encompass my personal philosophy on the *meaning of life*. They are organized around the 12 Universal Rules.

Although these rules are deeply and firmly fixed in my consciousness, it is not my intent to present them as dogma; but instead, I hope to stimulate your thinking on the nature of your "true" reality.

It also is not my purpose to provide a detailed technical and philosophical analysis. Instead, I offer a summary of what I have discussed elsewhere, enhanced by my complementary insights and analyses.[7]

In the interest of making this book more readily digestible, I have purposely omitted nearly all of the details of the relevant science. Therefore, I offer you a path for your life which you must take on faith, in the event you choose not to venture beyond this book to study its scientific foundations. However, if you absorb the messages presented, and if they resonate with you, then they definitely have the power to deliver. They have worked for me and for others who have chosen this same path.

There is a subtle but important point here. A number of the rules and axioms that I will disclose and discuss cannot at this time be proven by the laws of modern science, and in particular, by highly respected scientific methods, even quantum physics. They, in fact, fall in the realm of an emerging new discipline called Spiritual Physics. This is the last stage of human-based science as we have transitioned over the last 500 years from Galileo to Newton to Einstein and Plank.

Although the vast part of my life in science has strictly and faithfully followed the rules of the scientific method, I have learned to take a simple, but pragmatic view on those premises that cannot be proven scientifically at this time. I follow the *Cinderella axiom,* "If the shoe fits wear it!" If the concepts, rules and tenets of Spiritual Physics truly work when practiced as I describe in this book, why not accept and use them for the betterment of your life and for those of others? Their scientific underpinnings will follow in due time.

Should you be interested in more technical detail, especially specific relationships between quantum physics and consciousness, and the importance of quantum concepts such as *Entanglement* and the *Observer Effect,* you may wish to consult the references I provide throughout this book, as well as entries cited in the bibliography. The discussion in many of these references is, for the most part, presented in simple technical terms and hopefully comprehensible and digestible by interested laypersons.

In *Part II: Using The 12 Universal Rules to Create the Life You Dream,* I present practical use of the theory from Part I and address how to lead a fulfilling life based on the 12 Universal Rules. Here I explain in some detail how to become adept at relaxation and meditation and how to use these tools to uncover your Life Purpose, thereby providing tools to create the long-term personal and professional fulfillment you seek.

I also pursue in great detail the means to use the three fundamental elements of consciousness to manifest into your life those things that will help you unfold the reality of your dreams to create a fulfilling life.

It has been my experience that many authors who write about manifestation present it as primarily requiring a positive vision and attitude. In Part II you will learn that this is not sufficient for consistent successful manifestation. There are five distinct and separate steps to follow, and if one of the steps is eliminated or not practiced accurately, your manifestation may be unsuccessful.

What You Can Learn From This Book
At a minimum, you can learn the following:

1. The world you perceive with your five senses has definitively been proven to be an illusion. Understanding the nature of this illusion gives you the power to create the life you desire.
2. There are three distinct, yet paradoxically, intimately enmeshed levels of consciousness—Personal Consciousness, Collective Consciousness, and Cosmic Consciousness.[8]
3. You create what you observe in your five-sense world by the way in which you focus your Personal Consciousness.
4. Through your awareness of how these three levels of consciousness function, you can literally bring anything you

wish into your life, if you follow specifically defined Rules of Manifestation.

5. Using the Rules of Manifestation and an understanding of the path to fulfillment, you can create the personal and professional life you desire, and therefore, long-term happiness.

A Personal Disclaimer

I wish to acknowledge upfront that while the content of this monograph is not based on any tenets of organized religion; it is unquestionably deeply spiritual in its nature and context. This means that it has little to say about theology as expressed by organized religions, but much to say about spirituality—the non-material realm that extends infinitely and eternally beyond the material perception of our five senses. More to the point, the philosophy discussed here is generally antithetical to the teachings of organized religion.

I like the following definition. *Spirituality is a process of personal transformation oriented on subjective experience and psychological growth independent of any specific religious context.*[9]

The concept of God is used throughout, but this should not be confused with the God embraced by organized religion. The latter is certainly cast as omniscient, omnipotent and omnipresent. However, paradoxically, He—and it is most definitely and consistently presented as a "He"—is also merciful, yet judgmental; loving, yet retributive; and a provider of free will, yet in complete control.[10] Many envision Him as a powerful, all-knowing, white-bearded spiritual "person" sitting on a throne in heaven and pulling strings to manage things here on Earth. This picture has no relevance to the content of this book.

God, as used in the current text, is a genderless Universal Intelligence, a Cosmic Consciousness, and as you will hopefully see, is completely and intimately part of you.

I have purposely and almost consistently throughout the text used the word "God" in conjunction with Cosmic Consciousness, and not as a stand-alone label because I did not want to support the widespread concept of duality, namely that you and God are two separate entities. I believe that duality has done much damage to our civilization and more often than not, has held back humanity from reaching its ultimate potential.

The intimate fusion of Cosmic Consciousness with our own Personal Consciousness provides each of us with complete free will and the power to achieve things in a simpler manner, not understood or appreciated by most.

I humbly suggest that you contemplate and "consume" the thoughts presented here, just as you would a vintage wine with a gourmet meal—slowly, purposefully, discerningly and with keen observation of your experience as you digest them. In that way, you can decide whether the "wine" is a good vintage, or just "interesting." That's the word I sometimes share with the restaurant waiter in the presence of my dinner guests. It's my polite description of an ordinary vintage. What you ultimately conclude about the "taste" of what you read here, I propose, is your own personal truth, and hopefully that's all that will really matter to you.

As someone who spent a good part of my life in scientific research as well as in the business of using science to create commercially useful technology, I deeply understand the human need and desire for proof ascertained through scientific methods. However, such proof will not be possible until all of the laws of Spiritual Physics are known. Like you, I yearn for this proof to be available to all. It may well be the best path to a peaceful and sustainable future for humanity.

The "proof" here is in consistent positive outcomes from the proposed practices offered in this book. Followed diligently and faithfully, the specific guidance offered in Part II really works. It has been proven time and again, not just by me, but by many who came before me. All I have tried to do is pull together the salient elements of this "spiritual science" and present them to you in a way that can be easily applied.

These insights have taken some time to unfold and clarify within my mind. Yet, having spent several decades on my personal journey to formulate the 12 Universal Rules of Life, I believe that it was time very well spent. I continue to lean on the words of the philosopher Søren Kierkegaard: "Life must be lived forward, but can only be understood backwards."

I truly believe that those of us approaching our sunset years, and who have consistently looked "backwards" during our journey, do have something to share that can be of significant value to those of you early on in your path of life discovery. In fact, I firmly believe it is our obligation to share this information and perspective.

I would like to think that this monograph is not considered a "New Age" product, even though some of my physicist colleagues will take exception to this point. To be a bit facetious yet frank, the rules, axioms and insights presented here were not channeled from a supernatural entity in an alternate universe. I have tried to combine without bewildering scientific justification, the findings and insights of modern quantum physics with well-proven metaphysical practices of the Eastern Wisdom Traditions. This is the arena in which the early stages of Spiritual Physics are unfolding. I hope I have succeeded.

Even if you disagree with some of the ideas offered here, perhaps they will stimulate your thinking and analysis, and give you comfort with your personal truth. I encourage you to proceed intently from Part I to Part II: "try it on and see if it fits." I believe that you may be surprised despite not being able to prove and justify everything using the laws and axioms of our current knowledge of science.

This is the first day of the rest of your life. Why not create a *Beautiful Life*, the one you dream?

Enjoy your journey,
Jim Cusumano
Prague
October 2015

PART 1

THE REASON FOR YOUR EXISTENCE
—12 UNIVERSAL RULES OF LIFE —

*"The path within is
One that many
May travel,
But few do
Journey."* [3]

3 George William Russell, *The Candle of Vision*, The Library of Alexandria, 1918.

CHAPTER ONE
CONSCIOUSNESS IS EVERYTHING

"We are led to believe a lie,
When we see with and not through the eye
That was born in a night, to perish in a night,
While the soul slept in beams of light."[11]
—**William Blake (1757-1827), English Poet**

Cosmic Consciousness

To understand your true reality and why you are here at this point in time and space on planet Earth, I believe we must first define what some philosophers call Cosmic Consciousness. Theologians would be happier with the term God. Because of ambiguities, if not stigmas created over the ages by organized religions, I will generally use the philosophical term, although, when necessary to make a point concerning the true essence of God, I will resort to the theological term.

However, in the end it really doesn't matter. Labels are irrelevant. All that matters is what "speaks" to you. Cosmic Consciousness—God—is intimately and eternally enmeshed with your Personal Consciousness. In other words, God is within you, or as the ancient Eastern Wisdom Traditions teach, God exclaims, "I am That; and you are That, as well."

Cosmic Consciousness is an energy field that functions by laws of a science that are well beyond our knowledge of quantum physics. Only now are we beginning to get a foothold on this amazing science of the intangible, of the infinite, of the spirit. There are an ever-increasing number of brilliant scientists and philosophers who are awakening to, and participating in this emerging field of Spiritual Physics. They are pioneers who are comfortable with one foot in the science of quantum physics and the other in the philosophy of metaphysics.

In some ways, we are returning to the methods of ancient alchemy, when science and philosophy were united as one. They were torn apart during the Middle Ages with the birth of the scientific method and through great pressure from the Church Fathers that "Science and Philosophy should not be mixed!" Recall poor Galileo Galilei or worse yet, his colleague Bruno Giordano, who was burned at the stake by the "Holy Inquisition" Fathers!

These scientists and philosophers are uncovering the nature of what appears to most of us as "miracles." However, what we call a "miracle" is just a five-sense observable physical occurrence which our current level of scientific and intellectual development cannot explain. Our grandparents may well have considered a Boeing 747, your iPad, or many of our modern scientific technologies as mystical and miraculous.

Over the last 450 years, we have progressively moved from Galilean Physics to Newtonian Physics to Quantum Physics, and now we are entering the last quadrant of the sphere of human science—*Spiritual Physics.*

As this new science of Spiritual Physics unfolds, it will enable us to comprehend and increasingly participate in the creation of what we now see as miraculous transformations, both externally, and more importantly, internally. This is something Wisdom Seekers of the East knew millennia ago, but somehow disappeared from our conscious recognition as the presence and power of our ego increased and the noise of a highly interconnected world masked true reality.

Although quantum physics unquestionably points us in the right direction to understand the meaning of life, the laws of Spiritual Physics go much further. There are real measurable physical phenomena that appear to be metaphysical in nature because they are not currently explainable by the known laws of science.

For example, how do two atoms, literally galaxies apart, "communicate" instantly, faster than the speed of light? How do our conscious observations create the universe that we "see" with our five senses? How can one atom or molecule exist simultaneously in two separate places at once, that is, until we look at the system to see this atom or molecule appear in only one place?

The 12 Universal Rules that I will present to you in this book are among the axioms and laws of Spiritual Physics to help answer these questions. They are pieces we have uncovered so far, and all are interwoven in some manner with consciousness. Used properly, they have the power to transform your life beyond all expectations. The first of these rules is:

RULE #1—EVERYTHING BEGINS AND ENDS WITH COSMIC CONSCIOUSNESS.

Cosmic Consciousness is a universal intelligent energy field that is infinite and eternal. It is omnipotent, omnipresent and omniscient. Its sole purpose is to evolve continuously and infinitely towards ever increasing collective knowledge, awareness, connectedness and Oneness. Our purpose is to facilitate and participate in the joy and pleasure of this infinite evolutionary process. This role requires both our physical and spiritual (consciousness) bodies.

Consciousness Evolution

Cosmic Consciousness is Universal Intelligence and its evolution is not towards "greater perfection." It has been, is, and always will be, perfect as you perceive it with your five senses, or in deep meditative awareness, all that "has ever been," all that currently "is," and all that "will ever be."[12]

Human growth and progression are good analogies. A healthy baby, toddler, teen and adult each have all of the necessary elements to live a fulfilled and meaningful life at their respective stages of development. None is better or at a higher level of "perfection" than the others. A baby could not function as an adult, nor could an adult do well as a baby. These are simply progressive stages of magnificence in our physical and spiritual life journey as the human species, none better than the others.

The mechanism for this infinite progression of Cosmic Consciousness is through the physical and consciousness evolution of all animate and inanimate matter and energy in the universe. Consciousness creates and "manages" all levels of reality; those levels that exist deep within hidden dimensions and are only accessible through deep meditation, as well as those levels we perceive as our observable "reality" through the limitations of our five human senses. Your thoughts, inspirations, creativity, movements, for instance, your physical, intellectual and spiritual progressions are made possible through the omnipotence, omniscience and omnipresence of Cosmic Consciousness. They come from the infinite Cosmic Consciousness and they return to it.

The practical questions are "How does Cosmic Consciousness affect my life directly? How can it serve me as a tool to create a better life and ultimately, be helpful as the means to enlightenment?" The answers to these questions follow from the essence of Rule #2.

RULE #2—THERE ARE THREE ELEMENTS OF CONSCIOUSNESS. THEY ARE SEPARATE, YET ONE.

The totality of consciousness throughout the universe consists of Personal Consciousness (yours, mine, and that of others); Collective Consciousness, that which is associated with the intimate interaction of all material entities in the universe; and Cosmic Consciousness. Paradoxically, all are separate and yet, intimately embraced by each other.

This connectivity is what makes manifestation readily possible. We are all part of *ONE*, and our level of *Oneness* increases as a fundamental element of consciousness evolution. We are not separate beings. We are "inter-beings," and our Personal Consciousness, or souls, are all mirrors of each other. This is why we must always seek to benefit the *Whole*, for in doing so we not only benefit our fellow beings, but ourselves as well.

The Great Consciousness Connection

The consciousness that gives rise to your every thought and physical function is also the same consciousness behind all of the intelligent activity of the universe. This leads to the conclusion that there is no such thing as an accident or a coincidence. Each of us is part of the creative process of this ground of *Being*, for example, our Personal Consciousness[13] is enmeshed with the fabric of Cosmic Consciousness, which has no beginning or ending in time.

Thus, there is something much greater than we as physical human beings; and our consciousness—some might say our soul—is part of it, and it is an integral part of us. This is expressed by the words of British cosmologist, Sir James Jeans (1877 – 1946), "In the deeper reality beyond space and time, we may be all members of one reality."[14]

This observation on the part of Jeans is eloquently summarized in a statement by Neville Goddard:[15]

"In all creation, in all eternity, in all the realms of your infinite being the most wonderful fact is that . . . You are God. You are the "I am that I Am." You are consciousness. You are the creator. This is the mystery, this is the great secret known to seers, prophets, and mystics throughout the ages. This is the truth that you can never know intellectually. Who is this you? That it is you,

John Jones or Mary Smith, is absurd. It is consciousness which knows that you are John Jones or Mary Smith. It is your greater self, your infinite being. Call it what you will. The important thing is that it is within you, it is you, and it is your world. It is this fact that underlies the immutable Law of Assumption.[16] It is upon this fact that your very existence is built . . . No, you cannot know this intellectually, you cannot debate it, and you cannot substantiate it."

Goddard is emphasizing three critical points. First, God, or Cosmic Consciousness, is within you; you create your five-sense physical realty; and you cannot prove it intellectually—the proof is in the fact that all of the laws that follow from these points can be used to create a life of long-term fulfillment and happiness. As the Wisdom Traditions teach us, they ultimately lead to enlightenment.

Second, he goes on to say that "When we understand that consciousness is the only reality, we then know that it is the only creator. This means that your consciousness is the creator of your destiny. The fact is, you are creating your destiny every moment, whether you know it or not. Much that is good and even wonderful has come into your life without your having any inkling that you were the creator of it."[17]

Third, we must understand that all creation is done. In Goddard's statement the word "create" means that you have freewill to choose one of the many options open to you for your manifestation. In the world of consciousness every one of them already exists as vibrating energy fields. It is your choice to pick which one you manifest into the "reality" of your five-sense observable world.

So it would seem that regardless of all of the challenges you face in life, it is your destiny to achieve higher and higher levels of consciousness so that you can manifest into your life and the lives of others, more and more of the infinite wonders of this universe. The higher the level of consciousness you access, the greater your manifestation ability. There is no limit to what you can do with dedicated practice and persistence.

You can observe the power and connectivity of Cosmic Consciousness in your everyday physical being. From the moment of conception to the instant of death, it is the force that provides the means to orchestrate all that you do—everything without exception.

Your body is composed of some 40 trillion cells[18], a number that is more than 100 times all of the stars in the Milky Way galaxy, celestial home to our solar system and planet Earth. Every one of these cells, measuring less than 1/1000 of an inch (2.5 microns) in diameter, contains instructions within its DNA that would fill 1,000 books, each book being 600 pages long. Every cell performs nearly 100,000 biochemical reactions or activities every second, and each cell instantly harmonizes and correlates its activities with every other cell in your body.

This group of 40 trillion cells works as a team, supporting each other with all of the resources they have at hand. If not, there could be illness, and in the worst case, perhaps death. It would simply be impossible for a human being to live and function if there was not a mechanism for instantaneous communication and orchestration among the trillions of continuous reactions occurring over a lifetime in your body. This is one of the roles of Personal and Cosmic Consciousness.

Observed at the molecular level, more than 99 percent of your body is carefully and uniquely constructed by the forces of nature from only six atoms—carbon, oxygen, hydrogen, calcium, nitrogen and phosphorus—with a minute sprinkling of 19 minor, but very important others—sulfur, potassium, sodium, magnesium, chlorine, boron, chromium, cobalt, copper, fluorine, iodine, iron, manganese, molybdenum, selenium, silicon, tin, vanadium and zinc.[19]

If we were to assemble the appropriate combination and distribution of 260 trillion-trillion atoms (26 followed by 25 zeros), the result would be a 150 pound (68 kilogram) human being. An infinite eternal web of Personal and Cosmic Consciousness exists which can at its "will" assume operation of this human construct.

In the visionary words of French philosopher and Jesuit priest Pierre Teilhard de Chardin, "We are not human beings having a spiritual experience. We are spiritual beings having a human experience."[20]

Personal and Cosmic Consciousness also assure that larger superstructures like internal organs, body fluids and bone continuously communicate throughout the body in a way that enables the human being to function in a healthy manner. Yes, the autonomic nervous system "manages" all involuntary physical processes such as breathing and heart rate; but, the autonomic nervous system is under the "leadership" of Personal and Cosmic Consciousness.

Similarly, awareness or consciousness, albeit at a much lower level, is present in animals, insects, plants, and even bacteria and viruses. Some philosophers and metaphysicists believe that even at lower levels, awareness extends to "non-living" things such as water and minerals as well.

In this sense, consciousness is present in every atom, in fact, in every elementary particle, cascading down through electrons, protons, neutrons, and quarks. And who knows where after that?

However, it is important to note that although some level of consciousness appears to exist in all material matter, humankind is the first species since the genesis of life on our planet to have *total awareness* as a key element of Personal Consciousness. Thus, we are the first species capable of asking and struggling over deep questions such as those posited in the preface—inquiries such as, "Who am I?" and "What is my purpose?"

Non-Human Consciousness

Do animals, plants and other non-human organisms really have any semblance of awareness or consciousness? And if so, how "far down" to the cellular level does this awareness proceed? That's a question that has been asked over hundreds of years by numerous scientists. An answer may have been uncovered during research carried out over three decades, beginning in the 1960s.

Cleve Backster, a former naval officer during World War II, was a polygraph interrogation specialist, having founded the Central Intelligence Agency's (CIA) polygraph unit shortly after World War II. He also founded a reputable school in New York City which taught lie detection methodology to the FBI and other law enforcement agencies. He ultimately moved the school, The Backster School of Lie Detection, to San Diego, California, where to date, it has been the longest operating polygraph school in the world.

In February of 1966, Backster's secretary bought him a Dracaena cane plant to dress up his starkly decorated office in New York City. Early one morning, after working throughout the night on some polygraph experiments, he decided to see if his instrument could detect the instant when water fed to the roots of the plant reached its leaves. He reasoned that there may be a signal since the device functions by measuring galvanic skin response in humans, a phenomenon affected by water content. Those individuals not telling the truth emit more moisture through their skin than those telling the truth. Of course, the technology is more complicated than this, but that is the general concept.

Backster was also intrigued by research he had read that was carried out in 1900 by a highly recognized Indian polymath and physicist named Jagadish Chandra Bose. Bose found that plants actually responded to certain kinds of music and grew faster.[21] Backster's reported research findings were amazing.

He found that the plant did respond, and in fact gave a signal similar to that observed in humans. Backster was intrigued, and this set him on an entire new tack for exploring the use of polygraph technology. His findings were increasingly profound; actually unbelievable to many.

Even more baffling, on the morning of February 2, 1966, during his very first experiment with his Dracaena cane plant, as he sat at his desk after watering the plant and was waiting for a response from the electrodes that were attached to a leaf, he thought, "I wonder what would happen if I put a flame under a leaf on this plant?" But before he could get up from his desk chair, the signal from the polygraph instrument went off the recorder chart. This result was reproducible too! Perplexed, Backster thought. "Can the plant actually read my thoughts and in turn respond violently to my vicious intention?"

These initial experiments and many others subsequently motivated Backster to begin a detailed research program over a period of 36 years concerning the concept of consciousness and awareness in plants and other living organisms. Backster found that all forms of living organisms have the ability to respond to one another, from plants and bacteria to live foods and animal cells. For example, he carried out extensive research with leukocytes, the white blood cells of the human immune system, and found them to communicate with each other. He published the results of all of his research in 2003.[22]

Although early on, Backster's work was dismissed by many reputable scientists, recent efforts have found substance in his research results. An article in the *New Scientist* had this to say:

"In the past decade, researchers have been making the case for taking plants more seriously. They are finding that plants have a sophisticated awareness of their environment and of each other, and can communicate what they sense. There is also evidence that plants have memory, can integrate massive amounts of information and maybe pay attention. Some botanists argue that they are intelligent beings, with a 'neurobiology' all of their own. There is even tentative talk of plant consciousness."[23]

Professor Anthony Trewavas at The University of Edinburgh in the United Kingdom was one of the first scientists to seriously study plant "intelligence."[24] He cites the example of the parasitic vine Cuscuta, also known as dodder. In time-lapse photography, the dodder seedling appears to "sniff" the air looking for its host, and having found one that it "desires," lunges and wraps its tentacles around the host as a boa constrictor would around its victim. The dodder also shows a distinct preference for tomato plants over wheat. Trewavas remarks, "You'll stop doubting that plants aren't intelligent organisms, because they are behaving in ways that you expect animals to behave."

Cleve Backster's pioneering research was never taken seriously by the scientific community, primarily because he was not a scientist and often his work was not carried out with the best of scientific standards. This is unfortunate, as the body of his research was so large that a significant portion of his findings may likely have been directionally correct.

However, if you have any doubts about non-human consciousness, such as plants and their ability to communicate with humans, with animals and with other plants, and you would like to see a much more scientifically sound analysis, you might consult *Brilliant Green: The Surprising History and Science of Plant Intelligence,* by leading plant physiologist researcher Stefano Mancuso and science writer Alessandra Viola. You can also learn of similar findings from *Plant Sensing And Communication* by Richard Karban, Professor of Entomology at the University of California, Davis. Your view on the interconnectivity of consciousness across species may never be the same.[25,26]

Although we may have evolved to a higher level of consciousness than non-humans, there are indications, perhaps precipitated by the driving hunger of our egos for recognition, that unlike plants and animals, we have lost our way in our Collective Consciousness and its intimate connection to nature.

Eckhart Tolle[27] makes the point that "Nature exists in a state of unconscious *Oneness* with the *Whole.* This, for example, is why virtually no wild animals were killed in the tsunami disaster of 2004. Being more in touch with the totality than humans, they could sense the tsunami's approach long before it could be seen or heard and so had time to withdraw to higher terrain." This Collective Consciousness is present in all species, and to the greatest extent in human beings. All we need to do is to "wake up."

All of this work supports the contention that consciousness, more precisely Cosmic Consciousness is not strictly the domain of the human species. In fact, all organisms are connected. One cannot help but wonder, how far down the microscopic chain does consciousness exist? At the atomic level? At the subatomic level? The ancient master would say as far down as you can go.

The Orchestration "Miracle"

At the moment of death, Personal and Cosmic Consciousness disengage from our human "atomic architecture." Although these atoms are pretty much the same kinds of atoms that participated in orchestrating physical functions during the presence of consciousness, absence or disconnection of consciousness creates what we know as human death.

We are left with simply a lifeless pile of atoms to return to the Earth's composite—"Dust to dust, ashes to ashes." Unlike our Personal Consciousness, which is infinite and eternal, our physical body is but a temporary rest stop on the way to enlightenment. Perhaps, each of the atoms does have some level of consciousness, but this is not to be confused with human Personal Consciousness anymore than the consciousness of an animal can be equated to Personal Consciousness of a human being.

But while you are physically alive, imagine a single microscopic cell in your foot in instantaneous continuous "communication" with all of the other trillions of cells in your body until that microscopic cell dies and is replaced by another. And so it is for all of your cells. This consciousness communication process continues until the moment of death.

The fundamental question is how and why does this harmonization and orchestration take place every second of the day, every day of the year, year after year, until on average, after some 80 years or so of operation, it just "decides" to stop? The incredible beauty of this collective intelligence and instantaneous cooperation among all of your cells is beyond comprehension. Some explain it away by saying, "It's simply biological complexity." I don't think so. It is at a much higher spiritual plane than that. It is in the realm of your Personal Consciousness, your very soul.

Cosmic Management

Under the guidance of Cosmic Consciousness, your Personal Consciousness "manages" your body and mind as it expresses simultaneity and synchronization throughout the molecular structure of your entire body. In the quantum physics study of atomic and molecular species, this is called non-local correlation or *entanglement*. It's the ability of atoms and molecules to demonstrate their "atomic intimacy" by communicating instantly, faster than the speed of light, over great distances. In metaphysics, this is synonymous with omniscience, omnipresence and omnipotence.[28] This phenomenal effect is not speculative. It has been demonstrated and reproduced in numerous laboratories around the world.[29,30]

At first blush, the continuous communication among all of the cells in your body would seem to be nothing less than a miracle. That's how profound your spiritual-physical machine is! In fact, at a higher level of consciousness, one that is deeply hidden from our normal three-dimensional "reality," each of those countless cells is in some level of communication with all other cells—animate and inanimate—throughout the universe. All is connected; all is *One*. It is this connectivity that enables manifestation to occur quite readily.

A metaphor may help. To create a salt-water solution, you dissolve ordinary table salt in water. Crystalline table salt is chemically known as sodium chloride, white cubic crystals, which at the atomic level consist of alternating sodium and chlorine atoms extending shoulder-to-shoulder throughout the crystals as positively- and negatively-charged ions, respectively. When dissolved in water, the sodium and chloride ions break away from the crystal and swim uniformly throughout the water.

However, there are experiments that show conclusively the sodium and chloride ions as well as the water molecules retain most of their individual atomic and molecular characteristic properties. Yet, there are other experiments that show there is a collective interplay between these atomic and molecular species, wherein they act as one. So it is with Personal, Collective and Cosmic Consciousness.

All three consciousness entities are infinite and intimately connected, or as the ancient alchemists would say, they are "amalgamated into their Quintessence." As with the sodium and chloride ions, they are separate, yet intimately united! Your Personal Consciousness or spirit or soul—whatever you choose to call it—is infinite and cannot be contained within the geometric confines of a human body or within a lifetime. As challenging as it may be for us to comprehend, our consciousness penetrates the entire universe! That's why there are varying degrees of connectedness among all things throughout the universe.

On a personal level, and in terms of Spiritual Physics, your soul or Personal Consciousness is a field of infinite possibilities. It is omnipresent, omniscient, and omnipotent[31] awareness which at this very moment is orchestrating with simultaneity the trillions of reactions and changes that are occurring in your body.

Recognizing this connectivity and that the atoms making up our bodies were spawned in distant stars and ejected over millions of light-years across our universe, the late astrophysicist Carl Sagan was fond of saying, "The cosmos is within us. We are made of star-stuff. We are a way for the universe to know itself."[32] In other words, it is a magnificent means for the universe to look back at itself through your eyes—true Cosmic Consciousness!

We must dig a bit deeper to understand not only how consciousness works, but also how to use it in a practical sense to create a life of success and fulfillment. To do this we need to understand the nature of the mind and more specifically the conscious and subconscious mind. As the Buddha said, "The mind is everything, what you think, you become."[33]

Your Three Minds

Neurologists, philosophers and psychiatrists continue to debate the nature of the mind and whether it exists within or outside of the body. For our purposes, we will sidestep this debate and follow the path of Ancient Wisdom Traditions, as it all fits together beautifully, scientifically and metaphysically.

Unlike Personal Consciousness, Collective Consciousness and Cosmic Consciousness, which are immortal, eternal and infinite, the mind is mortal and it is space and time bound. And resides fixed within your cranium, the vessel that cradles your brain.

The mind begins to evolve shortly after conception and ceases to exist when the person physically dies. To be very clear, your brain did not create your consciousness, your consciousness created your brain.

Some elaboration may be helpful on this point. As discussed in more detail later, your Personal Consciousness is infinite and eternal and therefore constitutes complete awareness before your birth, during your life and subsequent to your physical death.

There is also a physical awareness, which is strictly the result of your functioning brain, and therefore operates only during your physical life time. This physical awareness is a result of a healthy mind and involves the conscious mind, the subconscious mind and the ego. It is often confused as the *seat* of consciousness. It is a form of consciousness, but it is temporary, and functions only during your lifetime. Personal Consciousness is your true, eternal and most powerful awareness.

Functioning of the mind is based on ever increasing levels of neural hard-wiring (knowledge and memories) that begin to occur immediately upon the mind's formation within the womb. This hard-wiring is primarily experienced-based, with increasing levels of mental content occurring as you learn from various sources. Your mind and thus physical consciousness is primarily associated with the thalamo-cortical complex in your brain. Most neurologists believe that this elaborate part of the brain is fully in place between the 24th and 28th week of gestation.[34]

About two months later electroencephalographic (EEG) signals from the fetus across both hemispheres of the brain demonstrate that the brain is now in a state of full neuronal integration. This means all your mental wiring is now connected. Scientists believe that by the third trimester all of the neurological circuits are in place for physical consciousness. The neural networks that form within the brain and make up the mind interact continuously with Personal Consciousness, Collective Consciousness and Cosmic Consciousness.

Intelligence, both IQ (Intelligence Quotient) and EQ (Emotional Quotient) are a function of three components. The *first* is due to a small level of knowledge "leakage" that has moved beyond the reincarnation "firewall" from past lives.[35] The *second* mode is from knowledge accumulated by our experience with various physical and spiritual sources. The *third* is due to the level and effectiveness of facile operation of the hard-wired neural networks, for example, how efficiently the mind's "hardware," namely IQ and EQ, function. However, all of these aspects of intelligence find their source in Personal Consciousness and Cosmic Consciousness. The mind then is simply a mirror that reflects this intelligence.

I believe the best source of Ancient Wisdom on the nature of the mind comes from the spiritual avatar, Patanjali, who lived sometime between the fourth century B.C. and the fourth century A.D.[36] Little is known about him and precisely during which period he lived because much information was handed down orally, until some centuries later when it was converted to the written word. Since transmission over the ages was strictly oral for a very long period of time, the fundamental elements of Patanjali's insights were presented and preserved as aphorisms, which are pithy observations that contain a fundamental truth. The aphorisms of Patanjali are among the most respected and frequently quoted wisdom over the ages.

He divided the mind (*chitta*) into three parts: *manas, buddhi* and *ahamkar.* Manas is the recording part of the brain, and it receives impressions and knowledge gathered by the five senses from the outside world. In our modern context, manas would be the resultant formation of neural networks throughout the brain where information is stored. Manas accepts all input as fact and makes no judgments as to truthfulness, morality or ethics. Therefore, in modern terms it is the subconscious.

Buddhi is the judging faculty of the brain; it is logical, and makes moral, ethical and truthfulness judgments and decisions. This is what we call the conscious mind.

The third part, ahamkar, is the ego which claims these impressions as its own and saves them in the brain as its individual knowledge. Because the ego is tremendously influenced and molded by social norms, I like to think of it as a product of social and cultural hypnosis.

In brief, the mind works something like this. You are walking through the park on a lovely spring day and you see a beautiful young woman walking towards you. You have seen her here before. Manas (subconscious) would say, "There's a beautiful young woman I've seen in the park before, approaching me." Buddhi (conscious) decides, "She is staring at me. She seems to be flirting with me." Ahamkar might respond, "I think she would like to meet me."

Patanjali would conclude that in this instance the mind process works this way: "It is *I* (Buddhi) who sees this beautiful woman. It is *I* (Manas) who believes she is staring at me and flirting." Ahamkar (ego) might conclude, "Now *I* know that this woman is attracted to me. This is my own personal knowledge which will cause me to introduce myself to her at the appropriate moment."

Patanjali also maintains that Personal Consciousness resides within, or more accurately since it is infinite, is associated with the individual. He calls it *Perusha,* and more frequently *Atman,* the word used today in Hindu scriptures. He says that the Atman is the real *Self*—God within us.

We often think of the mind as intelligent and conscious, but it is not. It has in fact "borrowed" its intelligence from the Atman, or Personal Consciousness and from Cosmic Consciousness—the latter is called *Brahman* in Hindu philosophy. Your mind simply reflects the intelligence and consciousness of Personal Consciousness and

Cosmic Consciousness, and therefore it appears to be intelligent and conscious.

The physical construct of your brain and therefore your mind determines how effective you can access the intelligence of Personal and Cosmic Consciousness. In this respect, it functions as a filter or throttle on knowledge. However, an accurate answer to any question you might contemplate resides within Cosmic Consciousness. In principle and in practice for those who are spiritually adept, if you can calibrate the throttle to the point of enlightenment, you could answer any question that is answerable. Some questions such as, "What is the precise nature of Cosmic Consciousness?" are not answerable.

When an event occurs or an object manifests in the external world, it is recorded by our five senses, and a thought-wave created by Personal Consciousness is generated in the mind. The ego always identifies itself with this wave. If the thought-wave is a pleasant one, the ego says, "I am happy." If it is unpleasant, it says, "I am unhappy." The ego falsely identifies itself with these thought-waves and this clinging to them is the source of all misery and dissatisfaction in the world. This consequence is summarized very clearly by Swami Prabhavananda and Christopher Isherwood.[37]

"The real *Self*, the Atman, remains forever outside the power of thought-waves, it is eternally pure, enlightened and free—the only true, unchanging happiness. It follows, therefore, that man can never know his real *Self* as long as the thought-waves and the ego are being indentified. In order to become enlightened we must bring thought-waves under control, so that this false identification may cease."

Yoga is the means to achieve this, and for our purposes, it is relaxation and meditation, two of the most powerful tools in our arsenal. Effective practice of relaxation and meditation can create a truly illumined person, one who is totally calm and at peace, even during challenging times of misery, disease and strife.

Now that we have defined the mind and its three primary elements, it is important to understand a bit more clearly the three fundamental states—the egoic, the conscious and the subconscious mind.

The Ego

The ego is simply the intense desire of our mind to identify with physical and emotional things, as well as thought forms. It is the basis for all duality. The ego reiterates over and over again, "This is me and that is you. We are different and not connected." The ego does not want you to recognize that the real you, the *Self* or the "I" in you is your Personal Consciousness. And it does not want you to know that duality is an illusion, for in *reality*, all is connected.

The ego behaves in such a manner that it in effect says, over and over again, "I am my car, my house, my job, my bank accounts and all of my possessions and outward physical accomplishments." This is, of course, the basis for our consumer society because we all want and need more to satisfy our ego.

The ego identifies with outward things and in the extreme this can lead to obsession and a compulsion for endless economic growth, as compared to spiritual growth. The ego loves *having* and cares nothing about *being*.

In the extreme, the ego attributes no value to anything that increases your true quality of life and long-term fulfillment. In this sense, it has sometimes been compared to a cancer cell. It has a blind voracious appetite for "more." It seeks to proliferate in the organism in which it resides, even to the destruction of the organism and thus, of the ego itself. It constantly professes, "I want to continuously inflate and could care less what happens!"

It's not that you should devalue the possessions you have, but when attachment becomes paralyzing, the ego is in charge and it takes over your actions and your life.

However, the ego is not evil. It is simply not conscious, which is why it is destroyed upon physical death. It's not in any way associated with your Personal Consciousness—your soul. Unfortunately, some of us don't realize this until our spirit is about to leave our body.

In this respect, I am reminded of the final scene of a film that many film schools consider the best motion picture ever made—*Citizen Kane*. This 1941 motion picture, written, directed and acted in by Orson Welles is based in part on the life of American newspaper magnate William Randolph Hearst, whose name in the film is Charles Foster Kane.

At the end of his life, as Kane lies in his deathbed, he struggles during his last moments and continues to mumble incoherently the word "rosebud." No one can understand what he is trying to say. The camera then pans back in time to his childhood and the sleigh that he played with during simple, happy winter days as a young boy. And there on the sleigh is written the manufacturer's name, "Rosebud." With all his accumulated money, power and physical possessions, the only thing that appeared to matter as he was about to die, were the simple happy experiences of his childhood.

There are two things that bring the ego under control. The first is simply recognizing when it is taking over and in effect, to catch it. Don't fight back, just observe what is happening. The ego fears being caught! That simple recognition begins the process of balancing the impact the ego has on your behavior.

The second thing that brings the ego under control is suffering. This is the basis for much of Buddha's teachings in his Eightfold Path. It is also the reason why some people, who undergo a major crisis in their life, often arise from it in an awakened, more conscious state and it completely changes their life for the better, namely they achieve long-term fulfillment.

Ironically, the ego is a necessity in our journey to enlightenment. It is by facing up to its power and dissipating its energy through controlling our incessant focus on the out-of-control thinking of our mind, and moving that focus to the Now or the Presence in our life, that we achieve lasting true awakening, both here and hereafter.

The Conscious and Subconscious

There are a huge number of volumes addressing the concepts of the conscious and non-conscious or unconscious mind. The latter is often referred to as the subconscious, however, many psychiatrists, starting with Sigmund Freud believe it is not a proper scientific term. Some, including Jean-Paul Sartre and Erich Fromm debated whether such a well-defined entity exists separately from the conscious mind.

For our purposes, we only need to understand that there are two important separate functions interacting with Personal Consciousness—the conscious and subconscious mind, where the latter refers to the unconscious mind. To avoid confusion, I prefer subconscious to unconscious, as the latter also infers physical unconsciousness. These two functions are considered major parts of human awareness.

Your subconscious absorbs everything that you experience with your five senses as well as any information that your conscious mind cannot at any given moment process to make meaningful and logical sense of. Your conscious mind is often not capable of absorbing disconnected information, as it could lead to significant overload and mental chaos. Thus, the subconscious stores this information until your conscious mind needs it and can make logical sense of it.[38]

The subconscious is the most important part of your consciousness. It is that part of your mind which functions below self-awareness. It manifests our circumstances, and most importantly, it is receptive to guidance from our conscious mind. One way of looking at it is *the subconscious mind is what you are, and the conscious mind is what you know.*

We must assume that which we wish to manifest into our life is already present until our conscious thoughts become our subconscious belief. Whatever we suggest with conviction to our subconscious is the absolute law that guides our actions, as well as the actions of others through the force of Collective Consciousness to bring forth our desired manifestations. Our subconscious is never objective or discerning concerning thoughts sent by our consciousness. Right or wrong, it accepts them as fact.

The subconscious reasons deductively and is never concerned with the morality, ethics, truth or fallacy of the premises that are imprinted upon it. It proceeds on the assumption that these premises are correct, and it seeks results and actions that are consistent with these premises.

Like meditation, hypnosis is an altered state of consciousness, and similarly, a tool to program your subconscious in a manner such that your conscious mind is completely and objectively unaware. In hypnotism, your conscious mind is put to sleep and your subconscious powers are openly exposed so that they may be directly manipulated by suggestion.

Properly administered, hypnosis is a powerful tool to instruct and manage the subconscious. A good hypnotist can hypnotize even a highly conservative person, make the suggestion that he or she will cackle like a chicken when a certain word is mentioned. The hypnotist then "awakens" the person from the hypnotic trance, and he or she enthusiastically cackles like a chicken upon the mention of the designated word. This entertaining behavior can then subsequently be erased by the hypnotist.

To my knowledge, no one has ever merged the practice of meditation with hypnosis; however, it may well be a useful means to help those who find excessive difficulty in "point-focusing" to enter the meditative state, a kind of "hypno-meditation."

It is critical to understand the relationship between the conscious and subconscious. The reason is that the universe and everything in it, including you and me as physical beings are manifested or objectified by the subconscious. Consciousness is the true reality, not what you perceived with your five senses.

Consciousness is the cause as well as the effect or substance of the entire universe. Your subconscious plays a critical role in creating your life, and if you are to manifest what is important to you, you must become the master of your subconscious.

Your understanding and knowledge of what might be called The Law of Consciousness—the mutual interaction and function of the conscious and subconscious—will enable you to accomplish all that you seek or desire to create a fulfilling life. Your conscious mind is personal, selective and judgmental; while your subconscious is impersonal, non-selective and non-judgmental. Your conscious mind is the domain of the effect, while your subconscious is the realm of the cause. Your conscious mind generates ideas and concepts and impresses them upon your subconscious. As your subconscious receives these ideas and concepts, it gives form and expression to them, never making any judgment about them, whether they are good, bad, moral, immoral, or whatever.

The subconscious never originates ideas or concepts. It always accepts as true those ideas or concepts that are thought by the conscious mind to be true or correct. The subconscious then goes about diligently interacting internally and externally to make these ideas and concepts materialize. This is why Einstein was fond of saying, "Imagination is more important than knowledge. Knowledge is limited. Imagination encircles the world."[39] Through control of your conscious and subconscious mind you have the power and freedom for true creation. Therefore, it is critical to learn how to control your ideas and feelings as they will enter the non-judgmental subconscious and be manifested.

Specifically, for example, if you want to dissipate all fear you may have about speaking in front of an audience, you cannot just say, "I will develop this capability," or "I have this capability." You must learn how to truly *believe,* and I would say even more powerful, to *know* you already have this capability. The importance of this concept has been articulated so well by Neville Goddard.[40]

"All creation occurs in the domain of the subconscious. What you must acquire, then, is a reflective control of the operation of the subconscious, that is, control of your ideas and feelings. Chance or accident are not responsible for the things that happen to you, nor is predestined fate the author of your misfortune. Your sub-conscious impressions determine the conditions of your world."

He goes on to say even more specifically:[41]

> "The subconscious is not selective; it is impersonal and no respecter of persons. The subconscious is not concerned with truth or falsity of your feelings. It always accepts as true that which you feel to be true . . . Because of this quality of the subconscious there is nothing impossible to man. Whatever the mind of man can conceive and feel as true, the subconscious can and must objectify. Your feelings create the pattern from which your world is fashioned, and a change of feeling is a change of pattern."

In effect, conceiving of an idea or a thought and impressing the idea or thought on your subconscious leads to manifestation or objectification of that idea. For better or for worse, we must always remember that our subconscious reasons deductively and is never concerned about morality, or the truth or falseness of a given premise that you may feed it through its interface with your conscious mind. It manifests into your life results that are consistent with the premise. The subconscious is in many ways the most important part of your consciousness. *Yes, the conscious and subconscious may be one, but your subconscious is by far, greater and more important than your conscious mind.* This fundamental truth leads us to the third Universal Rule of Spiritual Physics.

RULE #3—YOUR SUBCONSCIOUS CREATES YOUR OBSERVED REALITY.

The cooperative interaction of Cosmic, Collective and Personal Consciousness is the source of all intelligent activity in the universe. The intimacy, yet separateness of these three elements of consciousness initiates, orchestrates and terminates every physical and spiritual event that occurs in the universe. All is created subjectively by the subconscious with no judgment of morality, ethics or otherwise.

All things evolve from consciousness. It is this fundamental axiom that enables us to use the Law of Manifestation to create whatever we seek for a more fulfilling life.

The next step in human evolution is inevitable, and for the first time in our brief history, it can be a conscious choice. You can make that choice, as both Personal Consciousness, the true *Self* and physical consciousness are now conscious of themselves.

"I am That.
That
I Am."[4]

---

4 Exodus 3:14.

CHAPTER TWO
CONSCIOUSNESS AND REALITY

"Everything we call real is made of things
that cannot be regarded as real." [42]
—Niels Bohr (1885-1962), Nobel Laureate in Physics

Seeing Beyond Your Locale

Spiritual Physics maintains that the famous Mind-Body-Consciousness problem is not a problem at all. As Rene Descartes argued centuries ago, the human mind resides in the brain, and although associated with consciousness while a person is alive, they are separate entities. This is the same solution that numerous Eastern mystics have described over the last three millennia. Consciousness cannot be contained in the geometric confines of the human body. It is infinite in space and time and therefore exits after a person dies. [43]

Your Personal Consciousness is, as expressed by quantum physics, "non-local." This means that your consciousness is not present in just one place in space or time. It is present everywhere, and at all points in space-time. It touches me just as my consciousness touches you. It always has, and always will, exist. The intensity of your connectivity with others can vary significantly depending upon the level of your personal familiarity with them, as well as on which of the deeper hidden dimensions of consciousness you access. The former is why a person, through intimate relationships, is more connected to those relationships, but less so with strangers. The latter is why those who are highly enlightened and operate at deep levels of consciousness can often touch the spirit of the most remote individuals.

It is possible to connect more intensely with complete strangers and distant places by accessing them through the power of hidden dimensions of reality by means of meditation. This requires digging into deeper dimensions of the human psyche to access higher levels of consciousness.

This concept was the basis for the tens of millions of dollars expended by the CIA and the former Soviet Union in the development of what is known as "remote viewing," instantly "seeing" and accessing distant people and places. The term was coined during the 1970s by physicist researchers at the Stanford Research Institute, Russell Targ and Harold Puthoff, who believed that the technique could have great value for intelligence gathering. "Viewers" with a skill for deep meditation were trained in this process by these agencies. The fundamental premise behind this government-funded research was that human consciousness extends well beyond the confines of the human body.

It was the CIA's intent to use this capability to obtain top secret information from adversaries. However, they were unaware that this kind of spiritual contact adheres to the laws of Spiritual Physics. Love, compassion, sensitivity and a deep concern for the *Whole* are vital prerequisites. Thus, in declassification of the U.S. Stargate Project on remote viewing, it was stated that the technique failed to produce any useful intelligence information.[44] One must keep in mind that this information was declassified by the CIA, and it is doubtful that the agency would admit to any level of success in a public document.

There are innumerable anecdotal accounts of one twin sibling instantly knowing from a great distance when the other twin has incurred a significant mishap or tragedy. Similar examples abound with instantaneous long-distance connectivity between mothers and their children at the instant of a critical event. Limited intimacy between two individuals requires great levels of meditative focus as well as compassionate concern to penetrate the interference "noise" present throughout the universe, and thereby make a connection perceived by the human senses.

However, the connection is there, it always has been and always will be. The intense positive attenuation effect of interpersonal intimacy, compassion and concern is what often makes this consciousness connection possible without any meditation whatsoever. The combination of both elements—meditation and compassion—is a very powerful tool for manifesting just about anything into your life.

This connectivity is why it is readily possible to manifest your dreams and desires into your life as long as they are good for you and for the *Whole* and do no harm to others. Such manifestation was known and practiced successfully thousands of years ago within the Ancient Wisdom traditions. It is currently being rediscovered, repackaged and offered as a powerful new "secret." It is not a secret and it was the teachings of the Wisdom Thinkers that all people should have access to these practices. It is a powerful tool when used properly—"a path that many may travel, but one which few do journey."[45]

Our True Reality

Before we proceed further, I offer an apology because this and the next section may seem like they go beyond the domain of physics or even metaphysics and enter the sphere of voodoo magic. This is definitely not the case. We will briefly discuss the famous double-slit experiment and its results, which have perplexed scientists for decades. It is a clear point where quantum physics intercepts Spiritual Physics.

Don't be concerned if it is difficult to comprehend. Few, if any people understand the double-slit experiment completely. Even the brilliant Nobel laureate Richard Feynman confessed that he was baffled when he said, "The double slit experiment has in it the heart of quantum physics, but in reality it contains the only mystery."[46] Fortunately, the implications of the results are simple to grasp and that's what is important for our journey in this book.

Albert Einstein once noted that "Reality is merely an illusion, albeit a very persistent one."[47] He was making the point that we cannot understand true reality with our five senses. The only way to understand true reality is through the eyes of consciousness, or as some philosophers would say, "Through the eyes of the soul." Eugene Wigner, one of Einstein's colleagues, also a Nobel laureate and one of the architects of quantum physics, reluctantly confessed that "It was not possible to formulate the laws of quantum physics in a fully consistent way without reference to consciousness."[48]

The subtle point that Wigner was making is that the universe and everything in it, including you and me, would not exist without our mutual presence and our conscious awareness. Everything would exist as an infinite number of energetic vibrations, having no fixed physical form or appearance whatsoever. Thus, the universe comes into our five-sense reality by our conscious observation.

That is to say, everything in the universe is vibrating as energy waves. Only when something is observed by an aware being through their consciousness, does this infinite number of waves collapse and materialize to one specific observation. This process of the collapse of an infinite number of possibilities to one specific observation is known in quantum physics as *decoherence*. You can see how critical you are to the material existence of the universe as perceived by your five senses.

The Observer Effect

Modern day physicists struggling with this seemingly metaphysical phenomenon would say that an atom or even a group of atoms in a molecule can be described by a wave equation. Before you look at an atom, it only exists as described by a nearly infinite number of waves, extending to infinity. The moment you observe the atom, let's say with an electron microscope, the infinite number of waves collapse by decoherence into one wave that describes the atom you see. The implications are so profound that some scientists are now saying that the equation to describe the properties of this wave— known in quantum physics as the Schrödinger wave equation—is not simply a mathematical construct, but is a real part of our five-sense world.[49]

There have been numerous experimental demonstrations of decoherence. For example, it has been shown in various laboratories throughout the world that an atom or a molecule, the building-blocks that you and I are made of, can exist in two separate containers or places at once. Physicists call this effect superposition. However, the minute you open one of the containers and peek inside, decoherence occurs and the atom or molecule exists in only one box.

Decoherence also occurs in what is one of the most important of all physics experiments, the famous double-slit experiment. It is described in great detail elsewhere.[50] The profound results are as follows. A stream of particles such as atoms are fired at two narrow slits carved in a single metal plate and located parallel and very close to each other. The atoms enter the slits and are detected on the other side on a special fluorescent screen. They have the option to go through either slit.

If the physicist does not physically observe the atoms, the pattern on the screen is characteristic of a wave pattern, describable by the Schrödinger wave equation. That is, the experiments show that, oddly enough, each atom actually seems to "split in two" and go through both slits simultaneously just as a wave of light would do. Of course, atoms cannot split unless subjected to a high-energy nuclear fission reaction. So what's going on here?

The atoms are behaving as waves, instead of particles. As all waves do when traversing two apertures such as these two slits, they interfere with each other and form a distinct pattern on the detection screen, which could only occur from waves. You observe peaks of high intensity (greater light intensity) where they interfere constructively and valleys of low intensity (low-to-no light intensity) where they interfere destructively.

This is exactly what you observe when you simultaneously toss two small stones into a pond, landing close to each other. The water waves emanating from the impact area of each stone interact with each other forming an observable pattern of increased (constructive) and decreased (destructive) wave intensity, or wave crests.

However, in the case of the atoms, if the experimenter peeks at the atoms to see which slit they are going through, the wave pattern collapses to the pattern that is typical of particles. You observe a dark circular impression on the screen opposite both slits, the intensity of which is dependent upon how many atoms go through a given slit.

The correct interpretation is unavoidable. *Conscious observation creates this change from wave behavior to particle behavior.* In many ways, the double-slit experiment demonstrates the very essence of quantum physics, what some call "quantum weirdness," and a result that most physicists would rather not discuss because it smacks of metaphysics.

Quantum physicists call this the *Observer Effect.* As cosmologist, John Archibald Wheeler opined years ago, "The physical universe would not exist if it were not for conscious beings looking at it."[51] This concept bothered Einstein immensely. He was fond of saying, "I like to think the moon is there even if I am not looking at it."[52] He spent the largest part of his professional life trying unsuccessfully to prove that quantum physics is an incomplete theory, and if we could only find the missing pieces, so-called "hidden variables," then this apparent mystical behavior as well as the "spooky action at a distance" exhibited by the entanglement of atoms, would all go away.

However, in 1964, physicist John Stewart Bell, in a groundbreaking paper proved unequivocally that quantum physics does not have any hidden variables that would be necessary to make it a complete theory.[53] In fact, quantum physics is complete and is recognized by many scientists as the most successful scientific theory—ever. It has never made a wrong prediction and has been accurate to more decimal places than we could ever measure.

So you and I are part of this five-sense deception of reality. When we look at each other we see a three-dimensional anatomical structure that seems fixed in space and time. However, because the basic entity of our construction is the atom, which itself is not a physical object, our bodies are actually dynamic rivers of energy and information in ever-present vibration, constantly in exchange with all of the elements and forces of the universe.

In less than a year, you replace 98 percent of all of the atoms in your body with atoms from our universal environment. As the Vedanta scriptures asserted thousands of years ago, "Our bodies are just the place that our memories and dreams call home for the time being."

From all of the evidence presented here and much more observed in the halls of quantum physics, even modern science arrives reluctantly at the fourth Universal Rule of Spiritual Physics.

RULE #4—CONSCIOUSNESS IS YOUR TRUE REALITY.

Consciousness is your complete ground of being. It is your True Reality, not the mirage you perceive with your five senses. Your conscious observation brings the universe and everything in it into reality as experienced by your five senses. This is known as the Observer Effect, and without it the universe and all its contents would be a sea of an infinite number of energy vibrational waves, each characteristic of a unique possible universe and its contents. Your observation collapses this infinite number into one possibility, the one you observe with your five senses. This collapse to a single universe described by one wave equation is called Decoherence.

Several dimensions of consciousness exist within our universe. In addition, our perception of reality and our connectivity with others differ in each of these. In certain of these dimensions, our power to touch others is immensely enhanced. A very few individuals, who for whatever reason consistently function in normally hidden dimensions of high consciousness, can connect when desired with nearly anyone or anything in our universe. This is a very special gift. They are the seers and healers amongst us.

There are clear indications that as we continue our transition from what has been called the Age of Pisces (the last 2,000 years) to the Age of Aquarius that more and more of these highly evolved souls are entering our world. Some call them Indigo Children or Children of the Stars. The rest of us must access through deep meditation the hidden dimensions of awareness that are ever present within these children. Our ability to achieve such access increases with the evolution of our Personal Consciousness.

So we can see that the universe and absolutely everything we observe in it with our five senses is not true reality. This is expressed by the fifth Universal Rule of Spiritual Physics.

RULE #5—THE UNIVERSE AND OUR TRUE REALITY ARE NOT WHAT WE PERCEIVE WITH OUR FIVE SENSES.

The universe is an interdependently co-arising confluence of space-time events, omnipresent in infinite time—past, present, and future, in an infinite field of consciousness that is beyond space-time, meaning there is no beginning and no end. The universe encompasses all the events that have ever occurred, are occurring, and all that will ever occur. As incomprehensible as it may seem, all has co-arisen together. There is no such thing as time in the consciousness world, and the universe continues to arise and subside, ad infinitum into eternal Infinite Absolute Nothingness.

The fourth and fifth Rules are among the most baffling of the twelve. However, they are important because they point us in a direction where quantum physics will make the transition to Spiritual Physics just as classical Newtonian physics transitioned to quantum physics. And when this occurs completely, we will understand many of our most challenging physical and spiritual mysteries in our universe.

*"You are never
The same you,
You used to be."*

CHAPTER THREE
BEYOND YOUR PHYSICAL BODY

"There is a light in this world, a healing spirit more powerful than any darkness we may encounter. We sometimes lose sight of this force when there is suffering, too much pain. Then suddenly, the spirit will emerge through the lives of ordinary people who hear a call and answer in extraordinary ways."[54]

—Mother Teresa (1921-1989), Nobel Peace Prize laureate and founder of The Missionaries of Charity

All Is One; One Is All

Your Personal Consciousness never changes. It simply progresses over time towards greater unity with the other elements of consciousness within the universe and beyond. As a metaphor, think of it as a cloud of vapor made up, as all clouds are, of microscopic particles. This cloud of Personal Consciousness is thoroughly and homogeneously dispersed throughout infinite space and time enmeshed with two other infinite clouds, Collective Consciousness and Cosmic Consciousness. They are intimately mixed together, yet paradoxically separate.

It would be as if we mixed a cloud consisting of microscopically small black particles with one composed of small white particles. The black and white particles would still retain their color identity; however, the composite cloud would appear to be grey, the color intensity of which would depend on the ratio of black to white particles.

As the eternal process of consciousness evolution proceeds, envision "lines of a consciousness force field," not unlike the invisible field lines of force we can detect emanating from a magnet between its north and south poles. For a vivid impression of this concept, sprinkle some fine iron powder on a piece of white paper. Place a bar magnet underneath the paper and you will note that the iron particles line up symmetrically along the invisible magnetic field lines that flow in an elliptical pattern between the north and south poles of the magnet.

As in the case of the bar magnet, interconnected consciousness field lines form among the infinite number of particles within the three "consciousness clouds." This is a metaphorical picture of the march of consciousness towards ever greater levels of unity—*All is One, and One is All*—or, as Alexandre Dumas' three Musketeers would say, "*Un pour tous, tous pour un.*" All living and non-living entities move towards unity, singing together in concert one song, one verse: the *Uni-verse.*

You're Not the Same You

Your body is a whole different story. It is constantly regenerating itself. You regenerate all of the cells in your liver every 6 weeks, in your stomach lining every 5 days and in your skeleton every 3 months. The atoms which make up your physical being are not the same ones that were present in you some months ago. In fact, today, you have a completely different physical body than you had six months ago! Physically speaking, you are never the same "you" that used to be "you," not even five minutes ago!

Your Personal Consciousness is directly responsible for your memories, dreams, imagination, inspiration, intuition, insight and creativity. These elements are infinite and a part of the real you. They are eternal and outlive the death of your physical body through which you express yourself as you journey through your five-sense, three-dimensional world. So, in "reality," you are not your body!

Consciousness is our infinite eternal existence and our true reality. It is the only thing that exists in the Absolute Infinite Nothingness, which embraces the universe during its expansion and contraction to form and reform itself time and again, *ad infinitum.*

The concept of Cosmic Consciousness is congruent with Eastern wisdom and philosophy, which teaches the principle of karma. Namely, that we occupy our bodies for but a brief moment in time, reincarnating into a new body time and again until we have worked off all of our karma. The karmic process is not a rewards and punishment system, but more of an accounting means to be sure that Personal and Collective Consciousness in the universe continue to evolve in a direction that fosters an increasingly intimate embrace and connectivity with Cosmic Consciousness.

Reincarnation—Really?

I wondered deeply about the reality of reincarnation for many years, and must admit that I had my doubts for a long time, even though I had heard and read numerous documented stories and incidents that seemed to support this concept. But, as I became more acquainted with consciousness, it seemed to fit perfectly within the scheme of Cosmic Consciousness.

I ultimately became convinced of the reality of reincarnation when I recounted and examined my own history and it was increasingly clear to me that in a former life I had likely been a scientist, probably an alchemist. Allow me to share a couple of personal examples that support this point of view.

As a youngster, eight years of age, I was passionately attracted to chemistry and there was nothing else that normally interests youngsters at that point in their lives that even came close to my dedication to chemistry. By the time I was in eighth grade, I had devoured what was to be my high-school chemistry text and did all of the proposed experiments. I really didn't have to go to class by the time I was taking chemistry in high school.

Moreover, my real interest was in the use of chemistry to perform spectacular magic tricks for my friends and to create potent elixirs from the ancient alchemical literature. These elixirs were alleged to enhance your health and physical appearance. I believe that's why I created the various cosmetic concoctions that I sold in my neighborhood as a youngster. Ladies seemed to like my products.

Even though I studied modern physics, chemistry and mathematics in college, after graduating, I spent most of my free cash in antique and junk stores all over the U.S. and Europe purchasing ancient alchemical texts and old alchemical apparatus such as retorts and distillation flasks. I read the texts and studied the equipment for hours on end. I even had a small alchemical laboratory at my home. This was a very expensive hobby. Fortunately, most of my purchases were made many years before their real value was finally realized.

And now for the second and more mystical part of this journey: When I entered the research program for my doctorate, my research advisor, the late Professor Manfred J.D. Low, then at Rutgers University, told me that I would have to take several lessons in glassblowing from the university glassblower. My first research task was to construct a highly complex piece of glass equipment known as a vacuum rack that would be used to conduct our planned experiments. It consisted of an extensive array of glass piping, circuitous loops, bulbs, stopcocks and a glass ultra-high-vacuum pump, all extending from the floor nearly to the ceiling of our laboratory. This apparatus was intended to produce and maintain an ultra-high vacuum within the glass system that was similar to that encountered in outer-space.

One morning, while studying the design that I had created with the help of Professor Low, I experienced a strange and strong force nagging at me. I had an intense feeling that I could build this piece of equipment and did not need glassblowing lessons. I gave in to this pull and decided that I would try my hand at constructing this large totally glass ultra-high vacuum system. I assembled all of the needed pieces from the stockroom and borrowed the glassblowing torch. I worked all day and night, strictly on intuition, and at 3:00 am the next morning it was finished. Every joint looked as if it had been blown by a professional glassblower. I even annealed each one with a black soot flame as I had seen the glassblower do in his work.

But then, the acid test. After an initial rough pump-down with a crude mechanical vacuum pump, I began heating the glass pump to create an ultra-high-vacuum in the apparatus. I let it run and left for home to get a few hours sleep.

When I returned several hours later, Professor Low and several of the graduate students were huddled around my vacuum rack. "Who built this?" asked Professor Low. "I know that the glassblower is on vacation, so he couldn't have done it!" "I did," I confessed. "You did!" snapped Peter, one of the postdoctoral fellows. "What do you know about glassblowing?" "I just followed the schematic diagram; but it did take me quite a long time to finish," I admitted. "My friend," Professor Low said in a quiet professorial tone, "You either hired some talented person to do this for you, or you have a hidden talent much beyond what you currently appreciate." He then walked silently from the room. I am not sure he was ever convinced that I had built that vacuum system.

The second incident occurred about a year after my wife Jane died of breast cancer, when by a magical encounter in Ojai, California, I met at my home and fell instantly in love with my soon-to-be wife Inez. She lived in Prague and was visiting a mutual friend in California. When she flew back home, I immediately boarded a plane to visit her. Over our dinner together in California, I had mentioned my love for glassblowing and glass art, and since the Czech Republic is one of the premier places in the world for glass-blowing and design, she arranged for us to visit one of their famous glass factories.

After a tour, the guide said to me, somewhat jokingly, "Would you like to try your hand at glassblowing." He never expected my response. I said, "Sure, however, I have never blown large pieces from a molten mass of glass in a furnace, but I did do a little glass-blowing in graduate school, hooking together pieces of glass piping to create an ultra-high-vacuum system." He advised, "Well that's nice, but this requires quite a different skill." He was a glassblower, so I asked him to provide some key pointers, which he did verbally over the next several minutes. He then gave me a pair of dark glasses, put me in front of a huge furnace containing molten glass, handed me a blowpipe and said in his best English, essentially, "Go to it!"

I played with the blowpipe in the molten glass until I had a huge swirl of glowing glass on the end. I quickly pulled it from the furnace and blew with a steady breath, first intensely and then with slowly decreasing intensity as I formed a perfectly spherical orb. I did this by standing on a bench with the blowpipe extended perpendicular to the floor, thereby using the force of gravity to slowly shape the final piece. I used metal clippers to detach it while the glass was still soft and kept it close to the fire until it could be put in an annealing oven so that all the stresses and strains were removed.

The gentleman providing the tour was baffled. He exclaimed, "No one without training has ever done that. How is it possible?" To this day, I have that large green glass sphere sitting in my office, a fond memory of an alchemical flashback memory.

The Karmic Cycle

We can conceive of a simple metaphoric model for the karmic process. Consider a wide diameter cylinder that is infinitely high. It contains a certain level of karmic fluid, and the universal goal is to continuously increase the level of karmic fluid in the cylinder. This represents the progressive evolution of Consciousness towards Unity with all. Now envision much smaller cylinders of a limited specific height, the same height for every one of them, all surrounding the large cylinder. Each of the small cylinders represents a living person on Earth and contains a certain level of karmic fluid, which signifies their karma at the moment of birth. The top is open on all of the small cylinders and each one is connected to the large universal cylinder by a narrow pipe at the very bottom of the small cylinders.

Every time you participate in a negative karmic event, it violates the Laws of Spiritual Physics and works against the volition of Cosmic Consciousness leading some of your karmic fluid to evaporate into nothingness; but the universal cylinder "lends" you that same amount to keep you at the level you were at before the negative karmic event. It does this by pushing that amount of fluid back through the connecting pipe to your cylinder.

Now by the *Karmic Accounting Law of Checks and Balances*, you "owe" that much karmic fluid to the universal cylinder and must perform positive karmic deeds in your current or future life to repay your "loan." The more positive the deed, the more fluid you generate to pay your debt, and hopefully some is left over to continue to contribute to your own cylinder. As stated so well by Vietnamese Buddhist Monk Thich Nhat Hanh, "Every thought you produce, anything you say, any action you do, it bears your signature."[55]

The goal of every person is to eventually fill his or her cylinder to the top by performing positive karmic deeds, at which time the full tube of karmic fluid returns to the main cylinder, and he or she will have achieved enlightenment and completed the karmic process. You are reborn as many times as necessary to achieve enlightenment. After achieving enlightenment, there is no need for your physical body. Your Personal Consciousness becomes completely One with Cosmic Consciousness.

Thus, there is no reason to fear death, as your true reality, namely your Personal Consciousness, your soul, or your Atman is not only infinite in space, but it exists infinitely in time.

Your Personal Consciousness is the catalyst that facilitates and manages your journey to enlightenment. This is the essence of the sixth Universal Rule of Spiritual Physics.

RULE #6—PERSONAL CONSCIOUSNESS CATALYZES AND MANAGES YOUR JOURNEY TO ENLIGHTENMENT.

Personal Consciousness is not only your true reality, but also your infinite existence, and as such it is your spirit. Though not physically tangible, it is spiritually tangible. Your physical presence is but a momentary station-stop on your journey to enlightenment, namely perfect eternal fulfillment. So, by any definition, your Personal Consciousness is your true self. It manages your journey to enlightenment by the Law of Karmic Action.

So you see, you are not your body. Your true reality is your infinite eternal Personal Consciousness—your soul—which is an intimate part of Cosmic Consciousness, or what many people would call God. It orchestrates with great precision and simultaneity all of the reactions and changes within your entire body. Because your consciousness is infinite, all is connected, all is one. The singular role of all living and perhaps non-living species, is to contribute to and participate in the joy and pleasure of the continuous and progressive evolution of Cosmic Consciousness. In the words of quantum physicist John Archibald Wheeler, "We are not only observers. We are participators. In some strange sense, this is a participatory universe."[56]

Your spiritual journey through time to enlightenment is managed by the Law of Karmic Action.

I believe from the combined principles of metaphysics and quantum physics, Cosmic Consciousness is a projection of our human awareness, an indefinable entity that becomes more expansive and universal as it evolves. This evolutionary expansion is not towards progressive improvement because Cosmic Consciousness is already perfect. It is progress towards Oneness and Unity of all spiritual awareness and consciousness. To be sure, Cosmic Consciousness exists eternally and therefore before our physical appearance on Earth.

But in contrast to your physical birth, life and death, you must recognize that your Personal Consciousness always was and always will be, as it is intimately connected with Cosmic Consciousness. However, as your Personal Consciousness evolves over time, so does the presence of Cosmic Consciousness, namely God. You and God are thus intimately intermingled, and you play an incredibly important role in His presence and impact on the universe. As Eckhart Tolle beautifully notes, "You are here to enable the divine purpose of the universe to unfold. That is how important you are!"[57]

*"Listen to your
Soul ... and
Make the world
A better place."*

Chapter Four
Your Path To Fulfillment

"The more intensely we feel about an idea or goal, the more assuredly the idea, buried deep in our subconscious, will direct us along the path to its fulfillment."[58]

Earl Nightingale (1921-1989), motivational author

The deeper you connect with your consciousness through the practice of meditation, the easier it is for you to impact your life and the lives of others spiritually, physically, emotionally, as well as to achieve total personal fulfillment. Enlightenment takes a bit more work! In fact, meditation is a powerful gateway to finding and fulfilling your Life Purpose and Passion.

Life Purpose
You discover your Life Purpose by first finding that special gift you were born with. Each of us has an innate special gift; I call it your personal Essence, something you are good at and truly love to do. When you connect it to a Need in the world that makes it a better place in which to live, you have found your Life Purpose.

In doing so, you are facilitating the consciousness evolution of the universe. Your contribution does not have to be the likes of those by Thomas Edison, Marie Curie, Alexander Fleming, J. K. Rowling, Bill Gates or Nelson Mandela. It just must be based on three components. *You should be very good at it; you should take great pleasure in doing it; and it should make a positive difference in the world.* That's it.

49

When I was CEO of Catalytica Pharmaceuticals, I had an enlightening discussion with a gentleman named Jesse. He was one of the maintenance personnel at our largest manufacturing plant, located in Greenville, North Carolina. He was well-known for "whistling-while-he-worked." One evening, when leaving my office I saw Jesse whistling and intensely cleaning the halls in our sterile plant, where we manufactured injectible drugs. Government regulations demanded that the environment there be super clean and sterile.

I stopped just to say hello and while we spoke, I happened to asked him about his roots in North Carolina. He said, "You know, while I was growing up in the Carolina backwoods, both my momma and my daddy had to work very hard to make ends meet. So, after school, I was given the job to maintain the house, and I did it really well. I was good at it, and believe it or not, I enjoyed it. And most of all, I knew that if I didn't contribute, our family would be in trouble. So I was not only fine with it, I took great pleasure in knowing that I was helping my family."

I asked, "How do you feel about what you're doing here for Catalytica Pharmaceuticals?" "Well," he said, "I love it! You see, I know that if I didn't do my job well, contamination might find its way into some of the drugs we produce, and that would be a problem financially for us, and perhaps even dangerous to the patients who take our drugs. And you know, someday when I save enough money, I plan to open my own commercial maintenance service." Some years later, when we sold the company, Jesse did just that, and I have heard that he was very successful.

Sometimes jobs perceived by many of us to be at the "bottom-rung-of-the-ladder" are actually as critical as those considered to be at much higher levels. Doing them well with commitment, dedication and success requires a personal Essence, Life Purpose and Passion in very much the same way as being an effective leader or serving any other function in the organization.

Finding your Essence and connecting it with a Need that makes for a better world inevitably leads to intense personal Passion. As was true for Jesse, finding your Life Purpose ignites high levels of physical and emotional Energy. At that point, you will have achieved intense focus, and you will find that it's not unusual to skip a meal or go with little or no sleep. This Energy also unleashes high levels of Creativity.

In addition, the connectivity between the right and left hemispheres of your brain becomes fluid and super-facile. One result is that you will unleash well beyond normal human experience, a synergy of high levels of both your analytical and creative skills. This is the domain where great insights and discoveries are made. After all, success is not necessarily based on a high I.Q. Benjamin Franklin and Thomas Edison were not genius "whiz kids." They found their Life Purpose and Passion and operated in a state of high Creativity. That changed the world.

In such a creative state, you suddenly see everything in a different light. You are able to visualize solutions to very difficult challenges. All truly great innovators throughout history have experienced this energetic creativity—Leonardo da Vinci, Marie Curie, Harriet Beecher Stowe, Isaac Newton, Coco Chanel and Alexander Graham Bell, among many others. All found their Life Purpose, Passion, Creativity, and in this innovative state, the means to a fulfilling life.

With this power, you experience the generation of a huge Innovative output. You can create products and projects of value that under normal circumstances would not have been possible. The outcome is a Reward. It may be financial, emotional, psychological, spiritual, or some combination of these. The result is that you experience a deep sense of Gratitude, which is always the source of all lasting Fulfillment. The path may be summarized as follows:

—The Path To Fulfillment—
Essence → Need → Life Purpose → Passion → Energy →
Creativity → Innovation → Reward →
Gratitude →
FULFILLMENT

If you have ever experienced this path to Fulfillment, you will likely understand that much of the force for this process is powered by your Passion, namely enthusiasm for what you are doing. Interestingly, the word enthusiasm is derived from the ancient Greek stems *en* and *theos*, the latter meaning God. And the related Greek word *enthousiazein* means "to be possessed by God." So, in this process, you connect with your very core, your Personal Consciousness, which is God within you. You essentially have to do nothing to succeed in this state of *being*, simply ride the crest of creative energy you have raised within yourself.

Thus, it is important to understand that the Fulfillment you experience does not come from what you do in following this path, but rather it flows from your soul, your Personal Consciousness, into what you do, and therefore into the world making it a better place for all. The more people who practice this path, the more rapidly the Collective Consciousness of humanity will raise its head and bring about workable solutions for the vital global challenges we currently face and for a sustainable future for all.

If you have any doubt about the power of gratitude to induce long-term fulfillment and happiness, I suggest that you view a six-minute film on gratitude by world-famous filmmaker Louie Schwartzberg with orchestral composition and conducting by music impresario Gary Malkin, and narration by Brother David Steindl-Rast. Viewing this short film has been said to be a life-changing experience for a number of people.[59]

This path is always driven by a strong spiritual force, never by the quest for great sums of money and power, stature or position. It is based on an evolving new definition of success, one that is much more powerful and fulfilling than the old model.

The process starts with your Essence, which is firmly imbedded in your Personal Consciousness, known in Hindu philosophy as the *Self*. In the Bhagavad Gita, Lord Krishna advises Arjuna, "Your *Self* cannot be pierced by weapons or burned by fire; water cannot wet it; nor can the wind dry it. Your Self cannot be pierced or burned, made wet or dry. It is everlasting and infinite, standing on the motionless foundations of eternity. Your *Self* is unmanifested, beyond all thought, beyond all change."[60] So, if you have not yet found your Essence, you still can do so. It will change your life and very likely, the lives of others around you forever!

Your Personal Consciousness is the single force that can ultimately lead you to long-term personal and professional fulfillment. This is expressed by the seventh Universal Rule of Spiritual Physics.

RULE #7—CONSCIOUSNESS PRESCRIBES YOUR PATH TO YOUR FULFILLMENT IN THE PHYSICAL WORLD.

Your ability to experience long-term joy and happiness in the five-sense physical world is intimately connected to and guided by your Personal Consciousness, and can be described by a simple, but profound path known as the Path to Fulfillment.

The Power of Purpose and Passion

I have seen this path succeed numerous times for men and women I have known. I offer an example from my own life, as it is one I clearly understand intimately. It is a story of how science and technology captured my personal passion and changed my life for the better.

At the ripe age of eight years, I was a typical boy playing "cowboys and Indians," and exploring the local swamplands where I grew up in Elizabeth, New Jersey, adjacent to what eventually would become the runways for Newark International Airport. I hadn't the foggiest idea that I had a skill or passion for science—that is, until my parents bought me a chemistry set for my eighth Christmas.

I dove into the laboratory experiments book that accompanied the set and carried out nearly every experiment. It was all I wanted to do. I was hooked, mesmerized by what I could do with chemistry, even though I could barely read and pronounce such names as sodium ferrocyanide or ferrous ammonium chloride, both primary ingredients to make the most beautiful royal blue ink. I set up a small lab in the cellar of my grandparents' home, where I lived at the time with my parents and my soon-to-be three brothers and six sisters.

Yes, there were 10 of us, plus my parents, squeezed into the ground apartment of a two-family home. With our only comparison being Ricky Nelson's home on the TV show *The Adventures of Ozzie and Harriet*, we really had no idea how tight things were!

The Benedictine nuns at Blessed Sacrament, where I attended grammar school, strongly encouraged us to visit the local library and check out books that we enjoyed reading. At the tender age of 10, during one of my weekly excursions to the library, I discovered a book entitled *1000 Useful Formulas*. It contained recipes for making inks, adhesives, cosmetics and many more "useful" chemistry-based products. I started making some of these products in my lab, and packaging and selling them in my neighborhood under the brand O & O Research Laboratories. "O" stood for organic, the branch of chemistry I was intrigued by at the time.

The fact that someone was willing to pay for a "product" that I had "manufactured" with my "technology" fueled an incredible personal passion and set me on a trajectory of a life-long love for the use of science and technology to create a better world. What caused this amazing self discovery, one that would help shape the rest of my life? I had found something I was good at, loved to do, and I seemed to be making a positive difference.

By that single "act of the Universe"—a gift of a chemistry set—I had found my Essence at an early age and pursued it without ever thinking about making lots of money or gaining a position of power. Both of these eventually came my way, but they were a consequence of following my Life Purpose with Passion and wanting to do something that could make a positive difference in the world.

Of course, it didn't hurt that I grew up during the *Sputnik* / NASA era, when science was looked upon as a noble profession that could solve many of our global problems. I often wonder, "What if I had a special artistic skill and wanted to be an artist as a profession? Would well-intentioned forces that most often help shape the future of a child—parents, teachers, friends, relatives, and the media—have been supportive?" That is not only a fundamental question, but often a challenging issue.

In every known case of personal passion, success and fulfillment, the trail always leads back to a supportive universe namely Cosmic Consciousness. If this is true, then why does study after study conclude that the majority of people are unhappy in their job, and obviously lacking personal fulfillment? For example, a recent study by Towers & Watson of more than 32,000 workers shows that only about one-third of employees are happy in their job.[61]

I believe that there are two primary reasons, which are often interconnected. First, our archaic definition of success, based on only money and power, often influences children at an early age to abandon their Essence, especially if it is not projected to result in a profession that brings about this wealth and influence. Thus, it is a struggle for those children gifted with skills in the arts, sports, music, theater, philosophy and numerous other fields. As a consequence, we sometimes encounter, for example, "successful" bankers, lawyers and doctors who can't wait to retire so they can pursue their true love in the arts, or some other endeavor considered a risky professional pursuit based on our current model for success.

Second, we live in an intensely connected world, one that is filled with constant noise and trivial, meaningless distractions such as Internet games, reality TV shows, and senseless violence and gratuitous sex, permeating a good deal of our media. The information and content of these distractions strongly support the archaic defining elements of success—*money* and *power.* We are constantly bombarded by subtle and more often, not-so-subtle messages concerning the most "desirable" pursuits in this world.

Both of these influences are addressable on an individual basis. But, we need to do more. We should consider systems and information that on a larger scale address this deep "social hypnosis." Success could have profound positive results on the overall quality of our global future. However, the most dramatic impact could come by our redefinition of success and by supporting this new model on numerous communication and influential channels including parents, educators, business and the media. This new model for success is beginning to raise its head.[62]

Success Redefined

For hundreds of years and certainly since the advent of the Industrial Revolution in the 18th century, the pursuit of success in the developed world has been driven by two key forces—*money* and *power*. Think of them as represented by two of the legs of a three-legged stool. Unfortunately, for more than 200 years, the third leg was nearly non-existent, and therefore success was often unstable, off balance, and more frequently than not, a short-term event.

The new model incorporates the third leg to this metaphoric stool, and results in greater stability, longevity and unmatched human potential. And that leg is Purpose, specifically Life Purpose, almost always driven with a high level of service to humanity. By service, I don't necessarily mean an exclusive devotion to charities or nonprofit enterprises. Rather, we should support an individual's natural strengths and predilections, and help them find a means to focus their capabilities to make this a better world.

When you pursue your Life Purpose by connecting your Essence with a Need in the world that makes it a better place in which to live, you more often than not, make money and elevate your status in the world. Sergey Brin and Larry Page of Google, Steve Jobs of Apple and Bill Gates of Microsoft were not driven by a quest for lots of money and personal power. They all became billionaires and achieved positions of power. But, it was a consequence of pursuing their Life Purpose.

Steve Jobs is arguably an outlier. He was my neighbor for several years in Palo Alto, California; his daughters Erin and Eve went to school with two of my granddaughters; and so we spoke from time to time. His primary driving force was to make a better world by creating what he often called "insanely great" products. However, he had an immense egocentric insecurity and a need to stay in a position of total personal control so that he could make the decisions he "knew were absolutely necessary" for Apple's products to succeed.

I can tell you from my conversations with Jobs that he was not driven to make lots of money as his prime motivator. However, there was a strong ego force at work. He wanted to be known as someone who changed the world for the better. In fact, in typical Steve Jobs grandiosity, his perceived reach was much beyond planet Earth. He spoke often of making a "positive dent in the universe."

"All creation is done.
Look inside to choose
What you will."

CHAPTER FIVE
THE TRUE NATURE OF OUR UNIVERSE

"In the beginning there were only probabilities. The Universe could only come into existence if someone observed it. It doesn't matter that the observer turned up several billion years later. The universe exists because we are aware of it."[63]

—Sir Lord Martin Rees (1942-), astrophysicist
and former president of The Royal Society

Infinite Presence

Because it is intimately enmeshed with the cosmos, no useful conversation concerning consciousness can take place without a summary of the true nature of the universe and its connectivity to the awareness of all living things.

Our universe was born 13.82 billion years ago in what has become known in cosmology as the "Big Bang," an amazing expansion of what is mathematically described as a singularity[64] That minuscule point, unimaginably smaller than even a quark, which is the smallest subatomic particle we know of, was present in the "Infinity of Absolute Nothingness."

Nothingness here means no matter or energy exists in that space. It is the absence of anything and everything. This is a challenging concept to understand. It is not simply outer space, which still contains energy and subatomic traces of matter. It is the absolute absence of anything. Not a single atom or electron, no energy whatsoever, nothing.

Even in the farthest reaches of space of our universe, where every speck of matter appears to be absent, there still exists what physicists call zero-point energy. This is a consequence of *Heisenberg's Uncertainty Principle, which states that it is impossible to know precisely both the energy and position of anything.* Mathematically, it means that the uncertainty in any measurement of the energy of a particle times the uncertainty in the measurement of its location is always greater than a specific number know as the reduced Planck's constant. Therefore, if you knew the exact location of an electron, its energy would be infinite, and if you knew its precise energy, its location would be spread out over infinity.

In accordance with the Uncertainty Principle, subatomic virtual particles suddenly appear from nothing even in the deepest reaches of outer space and then immediately annihilated and disappear back into nothing. In this way, net-net, no lasting matter is formed, but the space is not completely empty, otherwise you would know its energy precisely. It would be zero and that's impossible according to Heisenberg. However, in "Infinite Absolute Nothingness," the laws of quantum physics no longer apply, only the laws of Spiritual Physics do. "Here," nothing exists—no time, no energy, no space.

Although beyond current comprehension, the singularity was but a minuscule speck that contained all of the energy and matter that would ever exist in our universe. "Infinite Absolute Nothingness" here refers to the absence of all matter and energy as we define them by classical and quantum physics, not by Spiritual Physics.

In the realm of Spiritual Physics, as incomprehensible as it may seem, the infinite presence of Cosmic Consciousness not only exists within our universe of space, time and matter, but it also exists within "Infinite Absolute Nothingness." It always has and it always will.

The Big Bang is actually a misnomer. This incredible event was not an explosion, but rather a rapid expansion that continues to expand in our current period of time. Metaphorically, you can think of it this way: All of the preliminary "stuff" that would ultimately become all of the energy and matter contained in our universe—past, present and future—was already on the surface of the smallest imaginable subatomic "balloon." And that balloon (the singularity), bathed in the eternal space of Infinite Absolute Nothingness, rapidly expanded into it from that subatomic pinpoint to its current astronomical size, and it continues to do so.

The result was the formation of all matter and energy in our universe. All of the galaxies and nebulae that formed as a consequence of the growth of this metaphorical balloon continue to expand in space away from each other into the cradle of Infinite Absolute Nothingness.

If all of this seems incomprehensible, don't be too concerned, theoretical physicists also find it difficult to deal with. While embraced by most cosmologists, it is beyond our comprehension. Our universe will continue to expand and evolve over billions and billions of years.

RULE #8—CONSCIOUSNESS IS INFINITE AND ETERNAL AND EVOLVES TO AN INCREASING LEVEL OF WHOLENESS THROUGH EXPANSION OF A SUBATOMIC SINGULARITY.

The infinite presence of consciousness has always existed and penetrates the universe, as well as the eternal Infinite Absolute Nothingness that surrounds the universe. Consciousness continues to evolve and progress ad infinitum through rapid expansion of what is called a subatomic singularity. It contains all of the matter and energy that has ever existed and that will ever exist.

The Universe Breathes

I believe that the universe will continue to arise, expand and ultimately contract to the singularity from which it sprang forth, and then arise again *ad infinitum*, proceeding through a process that has been dubbed the "Big Crunch."

Although counter to some scientific data cited by a number of contemporary cosmologists, I believe there is sufficient evidence that this expansion will slow down to an inflection point, at which time it will reverse over billions of years at ever-increasing rates of contraction until all matter and energy in the cosmos are recompressed into that initial singularity from which it sprang forth.

Those few cosmologists who do embrace the Big Crunch model, believe that this cycle of expansion and contraction has been occurring forever, and will continue this cyclic progression forever. In a manner of speaking, our universe is exhaling and inhaling over a cycle of billions and billions of years. In some ways this is similar to James Lovelock's Gaia Principle[65] as applied to the universe.

Recent research by world-renowned physicists Paul Steinhardt at Princeton University, and Neil Turok at the Perimeter Institute for Theoretical Physics in Waterloo, Ontario, supports the concept of a "breathing" universe that has been cycling forever and will continue to do so.[66]

As Buddha taught, "All things that arise will eventually subside."[67] Interestingly, ancient cultures of the Near East believed in a single and unique universe, which would progress linearly from creation to dissolution on the so-called "Last Day." However, the Wisdom Traditions of Egypt and India taught differently. In their view, the universe moves in endless cycles of creation and dissolution. As quoted in the ancient Egyptian *Book of the Dead,* Osiris, god of the afterlife states, "I am yesterday, today and tomorrow, and I have the power to be born a second time."[68]

Each time one of these breathing cycles occurs, Cosmic Consciousness in our universe and in the Infinite Absolute Nothingness has progressed towards greater collective *Oneness* among all aspects of consciousness. Progressed, not improved.

Modern cosmology recognizes that the universe is currently made up of dark energy (73%), dark matter (26.5%), as well as the visible matter we observe with our five senses, which is but a mere 0.5% of the total. Is it any wonder that human beings, when immersed in observation of the cosmos, feel insignificant? We currently don't know what dark energy and dark matter are. They are viewed strictly by our explanation and rationalization for measurable collective gravitational and energetic forces that exist and that can be observed throughout our universe.

I believe the validity of the Big Crunch model will become clear and more broadly accepted when cosmologists understand the detailed astrophysics of dark matter and dark energy and their inter-action with the geometric fabric of space-time and gravity. It may well be that these dark entities are made up of a completely new line of subatomic particles, whose properties make them invisible to our cur-rent measurement techniques. It may also be that there properties are an important link between quantum physics and Spiritual Physics.

These aspects of the cosmology and physics of our universe are very important as they form the basis for the ninth Universal Rule of Spiritual Physics.

RULE #9—THROUGH EXPANSION AND CONTRACTION CYCLES OF THE BIG BANG SINGULARITY, CONSCIOUSNESS EVOLVES TOWARDS INCREASINGLY GREATER LEVELS OF COLLECTIVE ONENESS.

The purpose of alternate expansions and contractions of the universe is a means to continuously evolve Cosmic Consciousness. This is God's progres-sive evolution towards greater Oneness with all.

Consciousness Evolution

We play a key role in facilitating this process over time; that's how fundamentally important we are. This means that our Personal Consciousness has always existed and will continue to exist forever. It also means that over the infinity of space-time, our Personal Consciousness, through the mechanism of reincarnation and the Karmic Law, has been associated with various animate and perhaps even inanimate entities along the way. For you, currently it's your human body, as the universe goes through an infinite continuum of formation and reformation cycles.

Therefore, we are all interconnected with each other, to all things in the universe and to Cosmic Consciousness, namely God, who resides within each of us. Our unity with Cosmic Consciousness increases with each expansion-contraction cycle of the universe, and with our own spiritual evolution.

Some years ago, at a presentation by the late Sathya Sai Baba, an antagonistic man in the audience shouted, "Who do you think you are, God?" Whereupon, Sai Baba replied, "Yes, I do! And you are, as well. The only difference between us is that I know, acknowledge, and accept this fact."

You might think of evolution towards greater *Unity* or *Oneness* in the following way. A man and a woman meet and fall deeply in love. Over time, the intensity of their spiritual connection or *Oneness* intensifies and continues to do so. Their individual personal attributes are not necessarily intensified. For example, if they are both compassionate, their compassion does not necessarily increase. What does increase though is their mutual sense of unity, a beautiful and magnificent sense of, "We are One."

In the terms of Spiritual Physics, we can say that each of these individuals has a certain level of spiritual energy. However, the combined spiritual energy of the couple is greater than the sum of the two individual energies. This is the power and beauty of consciousness evolution.

And so it is with the evolution of Cosmic Consciousness. It moves eternally towards ever expanding Oneness with all aspects of consciousness. What is so beautiful and profound is that this Oneness continuously expands, but never reaches a maximum limit—ever.

Over the last couple of decades, some quantum physicists have slowly and cautiously moved their thinking in this metaphysical direction. They have found that two subatomic particles or even molecules—the "stardust" we are made of—which have ever been in the vicinity of each other, experience what is called superluminal non-local *entanglement*. Namely, if one molecule experiences a change, the other "knows, feels and reacts" to it instantly, faster than the speed of light. It doesn't matter if the two molecules are separated by a distance of billions of galactic light-years.

And since all the matter and energy that make up our universe were once in intimate contact in a singularity that was the precursor to the Big Bang, *everything* is interconnected, *everything!* Thus, communion within the realm of consciousness among entities is always instantaneous, even over light-years or galactic distances. In a sense, *all is One and One is all,* and the degree of intimate *Oneness* increases with evolving consciousness—forever.

The absolute connectivity of everything in the universe is at the heart of the tenth Universal Rule of Spiritual Physics.

RULE #10—EVERYTHING IN THE UNIVERSE IS CONNECTED AT THE LEVEL OF CONSCIOUSNESS.

Each subsequent singularity contains the same amount of mass and energy as the previous one, but it is further evolved in consciousness than the prior singularity. It also has a cosmic "imprint" that leads to the continued advance of physical and spiritual evolution with each new cycle. This process will continue forever. Because all of the mass and energy in the universe was in intimate contact within the singularity before its expansion, quantum entanglement tells us that everything in the universe is connected.

Perhaps at some distant point in the future, the interface between matter and consciousness will have evolved so extensively that our physical bodies will be unnecessary for continued evolution of Personal, Collective and Cosmic Consciousness. That might well be birth of the *Perfect Universe.*

*"Before there was
Anything, there
Was love."*

CHAPTER SIX

THE FUNDAMENTAL FORCE

IN OUR UNIVERSE

"Nothing is impossible for pure love."[69]
Mahatma Gandhi (1869-1948), Political Activist

The greatest Wisdom Thinkers of humanity throughout the ages have maintained that love is the single fundamental force that governs all action in the universe. How can that really be?

What Is Love?

Love is difficult to define. The dictionary states, "A strong feeling of affection; a great interest and pleasure in something; or a deep feeling of sexual love for someone."[70] I don't think this captures it all, and certainly not its multidimensional web throughout the universe.

Love is not simply a sentimental or sensual gesture, or even a Darwinian sexual reproduction force among members of a given species. It is a pragmatically necessary universal force because all things, living and not, have varying dimensions of consciousness and all are universally connected and interdependent now and forever. *Love is the catalytic force that enables all things to interact for the benefit of the Whole, as it navigates its evolutionary journey towards Oneness of all. It facilitates the evolution of all consciousness.*

As with all catalysts, it lowers and often eliminates the barrier to a specific transformation, one that will achieve something of value in the universe that can benefit the *Whole.* Furthermore, in its perfect state, as is the case for any perfect catalyst, love selectively achieves only the desired goal with no negative consequences or collateral damage. The most impressive and phenomenal achievements by humankind have all had a definitive and necessary level of love at a key point in their manifestation.

The challenge is that there are numerous levels of love, but in the English language only one word to describe them all. "Use the word 'love' in a business environment—are you crazy?" That's the normal reaction by executives schooled in the old business model created some 250 years ago.

However, in Sanskrit there are 96 words to describe various kinds of love; there are 80 in Persian and 3 in Greek. In English, love can mean a broad spectrum of feelings and attitudes ranging from a simple pleasure such as "I loved that meal," or "I would love to help you," to a platonic caring observation, "I love the way she dresses," to intense interpersonal attachment such as, "I love her with my whole heart and soul."

The same word could also describe a process that occurs in your body when numerous cells go to the rescue of one or more of your cells running low on vital nutrients. These helper cells naturally share with their ailing neighbor what nutrients they can spare, so that they can assure continued health and function of the threatened cell, and most important, of the *Whole*. You can also see this process at work on planet Earth through the fundamentals of James Lovelock's Gaia principle.[71]

From a philosophical point of view, love can also be seen as a virtue, where one extols a sense of compassion, caring and kindness. Consequently, we find that in much of the Western world, this diversity in meanings for the word love often causes confusion and makes it difficult to define and communicate what is truly meant in a given situation. However, love is arguably the most important psychological concept and force in any culture.

In its various forms, love is the prime facilitator in all interpersonal relationships and has the most significant power to make things happen successfully. It matters not whether the relationship is one based on business or a passionate connection with your lover. This point extends also to interactions between non-human species, as well, even down to the cells in your body.

Therefore, it cannot be eliminated from your day-to-day personal interactions if you expect to inspire yourself and others around you, and to make great things happen. In business, the word love equates precisely to a sense of caring, compassion, trust, kindness, understanding and commitment. If you have ever been inspired by a person, you may recall that even though they person may have been demanding, he or she also had a deep sincere interest in your wellbeing and demonstrated the caring and compassion to support that commitment. What about the other side of the coin—selfishness?

Selfishness is a negative force in a world of selfless love. However, "compassionate self interest" is a positive force. Doing something for another because it touches and nourishes your soul creates positive karma. It is the perfect win-win. You help another and positive feedback to you follows. As so well stated in the *Prayer to St. Francis*, "It is in giving that we receive."[72]

Although selfless love is the positive force behind the beneficial evolution of the *Whole*, selfishness is also a form of love. It is love of self, and more precisely, love of ego. This kind of negative "love" is responsible for most of the negative forces in our world. As Eckhart Tolle reminds us, "You cannot fight against the ego and win, just as you cannot fight against darkness. The light of consciousness is all that is necessary. You are that light."[73]

Continuous evolution of forms of consciousness requires a level of personal elation. What could be better? It is mutual service among the conscious entities of the universe—"It is in giving that we receive." If one entity helps another, it helps itself and it helps the entire "collective" of species. This assistance is absolutely necessary for our Big Mission—our consciousness evolution and progression towards *Oneness*.

Love's Great Detractor

A deep sense of selfless love is innate and evolved to various levels within all species of the universe. However, due to social hypnosis and egocentric forces among more highly-developed organisms concerning their perception of success and their focus on personal status, it is often diminished.

Human beings are the prime example. They are easily distracted by learned, ingrained social behaviors, such as hoarding material objects, groping for power and disregarding the value of service or Life Purpose, for the benefit of the universal collective. Nearly all developed cultures create a predisposition for such behavior by defining success as being directly related to the level of two fundamental factors—Wealth and Power. This behavior completely eludes the concept of service for the benefit of the *Whole.*

Based on most social global standards and metrics, there is nothing innately unethical or immoral with Wealth and Power in society, as long as they are balanced by an appropriate level of service and in the interest of the *Whole. To be clear, by service, I mean the application of your fundamental Essence, something you are very good at and love to do, to a Need in the world that makes it a better place, essentially your Life Purpose.*

Recall the metaphor for the definition of success mentioned in Chapter 1 as a three-legged stool; the three legs respectively representing Wealth, Power and Life Purpose or service. Without a sufficient level of service, that leg is either non-existent or too short, and the stool becomes physically unstable, and tips over.

Tellingly, service that benefits the *Whole,* almost never results from a focus strictly on Wealth and Power, but Wealth and position or Power very often result from a focus on service. The lives of great social contributors such as Alfred Nobel, Sir John Templeton and Bill Gates are but a few examples where passionate service led to wealth and power.

Ironically, behavior that disregards social service does not occur among the most primitive of species in nature. For example, in a healthy human being at the microscopic level, there is never any hoarding of life-sustaining nutrients by any of the 40 trillion constituent cells that make up the human body. In fact, the average cell maintains only marginal levels of vital nutrients inventory to support its existence. As we saw earlier, should a cell run short and face the prospect of premature death, its neighbors gather together and share some of their limited supplies with the threatened cell to prevent its demise. This behavior of service recognizes and supports the collective evolution of the entire organism, physically and consciously.

The fundamental difference between a non-hoarding single cell creature and an "evolved" human being is the presence of the ego in the latter. One purpose of the ego is to provide a mechanism via a disciplined "taming of the ego" to elevate and evolve consciousness to higher and higher levels and eventually to *enlightenment.*

Love in its numerous forms is as pervasive as the force of gravity in the universe. Physical and consciousness evolution would be impossible without it. As such, this fundamental force forms the basis for the eleventh Universal Rule of Spiritual Physics.

RULE #11—LOVE, THE STRONGEST FORCE IN THE UNIVERSE, ENABLES ALL CONSCIOUS ENTITIES TO INTERACT FOR THE BENEFIT OF THE WHOLE.

Love is the catalytic force that enables all things to interact for the benefit of the "Whole" as it navigates the evolutionary journey of Personal, Collective and Cosmic Consciousness towards Oneness. Perfect love is a deep combination of the following: collective awareness of, selfless concern and compassion for, cooperation with, and a commitment to all other entities in the universe. For pragmatic evolutionary reasons, not sensual or sexual ones, it is the most potent force in the universe.

There is no other force in the universe that comes close to the potency of Love in its impact on and necessity for the primary goal of universal existence—the evolutionary progression of Personal, Collective and Cosmic Consciousness towards increasing levels of *Oneness.* It is the super-force that makes possible our eternal and elegant *cosmic dance* together.

*"The power of the
Sacred Feminine
Is beyond
Comprehension."*

Chapter Seven

Balancing Masculine-Feminine Energies

"The deepest experience of the creator is feminine, for it is experience of receiving and bearing."[74]
—Rainer Maria Rilke (1875-1926), Bohemian-Austrian poet

Although *Homo sapiens* have only been here on Earth for a very short period of our planet's total history, we have rapidly evolved both physically and consciously. Over the past century, we have advanced exponentially in our technological capabilities. These same tools have created unprecedented challenges for humanity. Nuclear proliferation, climate change, global pandemics, massive migrations and more are the flip side of this coin of progress.

A single element is required to manage our advancing capabilities in a way that does not lead to our demise, but rather enhances our possibilities. That fundamental element is a dynamic equilibrium of masculine and feminine energies. Properly developed and executed, this force has the ability to create a sustainable world for all, as far into the future as we can imagine.

Of the two gender energies, the one which has suffered the greatest challenges over the last 2,000 years is the feminine. Before discussing the means to a sustainable future, it is useful to recognize how our current state of affairs came about. It started most intensely and conspicuously with organized religion.

Religion

While organized religion has provided certain values over the ages to people in need, it ironically has in general created a significant barrier to the continuous evolution of Cosmic Consciousness.

Even so, although it has mitigated the rate of evolutionary progress of Personal and Collective Consciousness, organized religion has sometimes played a role in helping people find comfort, hope and occasionally their path towards personal fulfillment.

For example, my 93-year-old mother birthed and raised 10 children, and by all measures has lived a fulfilling spiritual life. As a devout Roman Catholic and through her meditative prayers, she sought to manifest for herself and others, small "miracles" to overcome seemingly impossible challenges. She did so by daily deep prayer and meditation to the Blessed Mother. She is a prime example of someone spiritually in tune, who has manifested benefits into her life and into the lives of others, long before the commercial popularity of the book *The Secret*.[75]

She was constantly sought out by friends and family to pray for their special needs and intentions. She found ways to see past the inordinate wealth and power games of the Church, and excused them as the foibles of misguided men and not the creations of God. I suspect that great saints like Augustine of Hippo, Francis of Assisi, Joan of Arc and Mother Theresa did the same.

We are also the benefactors of certain pockets of social good administered by organized religion. I would like to share an example that I experienced.

I attended St. Benedict's Preparatory School, an elite all-boys catholic school in Newark, New Jersey, from which I graduated in 1960. At that time, it was and had been since the late 19th century, a prep school for boys from upper middle-class and wealthy families. I was one of the exceptions, having been accepted through the kind auspices of our parish pastor, who had taught there in the past. My parents could not afford the tuition, so I was admitted on a financial scholarship.

A few decades after I graduated, the Benedictine monks who manage the school, became deeply interested in helping their distressed urban community. After closing for one year, they made the decision to change directions and reopened the center as an inner-city school accepting boys from the ghettos and poor districts of Newark. Nearly every student receives financial aid through funds raised by the monks, often from well-heeled alumni.

Their success has been phenomenal and has been dramatized in an excellent documentary entitled, *The Rule*.[76] Nearly every one of their graduates is accepted to college, many attending the best of schools, such as Lehigh, Swarthmore, Bates and Franklin and Marshall. Here again, organized religion creates social and cultural value.

There are some findings indicating that organized religion also may have played a role in jumpstarting the cultural and social evolution of humankind into the era of modernity we currently enjoy. For ages it was thought that some 10,000 years ago, our predecessors began what was to become the greatest transformation in human history—a transition from a nomadic foraging lifestyle to one of permanent farming villages.

We have thought for numerous decades that this Neolithic Revolution was due to a single factor, the need for an adequate supply of food. This was to have led to the invention of farming and as consequent byproducts—cities, writing, and then organized religion.

But now it seems from archeological findings at Göbekli Tepe in Turkey that religion may have been the catalyst for this Neolithic Revolution[77] A cluster of 11,000-year-old buildings with spectacular religious statues and monumental spiritual architecture suggests that they were built by nomads and not by farmers.

Some archeologists believe it was organized religion that drove the movement to farming and subsequent cultural inventions. Similar discoveries have been made in Central America regarding the Mayan civilization.[78] and in the Levant, a large area in ancient

Southwest Asia bounded by the Taurus Mountains of Anatolia in the north, the Mediterranean Sea in the west, and the north Arabian Desert and Mesopotamia in the east.[79]

Organized religion may also provide useful preparation for transition to the next stage of awakening which is consciousness discovery, wherein a person studies and becomes intimately in tune with the detailed nature of the cosmos, Cosmic Consciousness and the *Meaning of Life.*

In this sense, it highlights a historical and theological context for the avatar that is closest to your spirit and your way of thinking, whether it is Buddha, Krishna, Jesus, Abraham, Moses, Mohammed, Patanjali, Rumi, Dalai Lama Gendun Drup, Confucius, Lao-Tzu or any of the other great spirits who walked the Earth at a certain point in time. This exposure can have some foundational value, as long as you don't confuse and intermingle man-made religious dogma with the nature of consciousness.

However, despite these important social contributions, I wish to make an important point. *Although organized religion may have played a useful role in the cultural and social revolution of humanity, it does not follow that it has played the same central role in humanity's spiritual evolution.*

It is not my intent to malign the Church or any other organized religion. Yes, they have had their fair share of negative press, but by and large, the majority of their members are well-intentioned individuals. As it did for my mother, organized religion can provide some value to their faithful. It is, however, a historical fact that most organized religions deviate significantly in their dogma and teachings from the intent and wisdom of the original avatars upon whom these religions were founded.

For example, the early Christian Church Fathers reinterpreted much of what Jesus explicitly taught. History teaches that it was the intent of these Church Fathers to maintain control and power through fear and a stringent organization, which they did successfully by forming strong alliances with the prevailing government forces, for example, The Holy Roman Empire.

Another example; most Christian religions are based on what is known as the Pauline Doctrine. Essentially, Paul the Apostle reinterpreted and rewrote Jesus' messages as he saw them, and many scholars even today note that his writings were not the specific teachings of Jesus of Nazareth. It is well known and documented that a powerful 2nd century theologian and scholar by the name of Marcion of Sinope convinced early Church Fathers to follow the Pauline Doctrine almost exclusively. Marcion was eventually excommunicated, but the Pauline Doctrine remains to this very day.[80]

Thus, by and large, organized religion has contributed more than its fair share to detract from the universal goal of the evolution of Cosmic Consciousness. Great saints and avatars such as Buddha, Krishna, Jesus, Abraham, Moses, Mohammed, Patanjali, Rumi, Confucius, Lao-Tzu and others were human manifestations of Cosmic Consciousness—God, in our modern context. It was their intent and purpose by their presence and teachings to provide us with powerful tools to assist us in our journey towards the evolution of consciousness, and ultimately to our personal enlightenment. They sought to help us find a path to a fulfilled life, here and hereafter.

It was not their intention to create organized religions adorned with great wealth, magnificent temples and huge financial assets. That was the work over the ages of men who, driven by greed and their personal fear, focused efforts on wealth and power as a means to control the faithful and confiscate immense levels of wealth.

Formalized religions were most often formed hundreds of years after the death of the spiritual avatar, when many of the avatar's fundamental teachings were either forgotten, ignored or modified to suit the needs of those directing the growth of the religion for their personal benefit.

A perfect example is the expulsion of the Gnostic Gospels of Philip, Thomas, Mary Magdalene and others, about 52 in total, because they did not fit the story that the early Christian Church Fathers at the time decided was the desired one. Most of the written copies of these gospels were either destroyed or hidden in remote places.

Over the centuries some were found, such as the Nag Hammadi Library discovered in December 1945 by two farmers in a remote area of the Egyptian desert. These gospels, for example the Gospel of Thomas had been written shortly after Christ's crucifixion and are held by some scholars to be a much more accurate presentation of Christian history and theology than the Pauline Doctrine.

Rules were also set forth by the early Church Fathers to control and manage large numbers of the faithful, driving them towards a direction desirable for the purposes of the men who held the authority. I say "men" as there were no women involved in this power game. The primary goals were wealth and the creation and preservation of an incontestable position of influence. These early founders of organized religions were short on love, compassion and service. Theirs was the "carrot and the stick" strategy; heaven and salvation on one hand, and Satan, hell, and "fire and brimstone" on the other.

Historically too, some of the most violent wars have been fought in the name of organized religion. To name just a few examples, witness the "Holy Crusades," the Spanish Inquisition, the 17th century Thirty Years War between Protestants and Catholics, the Second Sudanese Civil War, and the "Holy War" of terrorism that permeates a significant part of today's world, tearing apart the true innate spiritual fabric of humanity.[81]

Avatars over the centuries never saw themselves as *the* God, but instead, as an intimate part of God or Cosmic Consciousness; which is how they saw others, as well. They never considered themselves as special. Recall Jesus' humble words to his disciples who were amazed by his miracles, "All I do, you can do, and more!" This assertion is assuredly correct, as The Law of Manifestation, with outcomes often appearing miraculous, has been successfully practiced by many.

Thus, we find that historically, organized religion played a key role in elevating masculine energies most often at the demise of feminine energies.

The Sacred Feminine

Long-term success of any culture requires an optimal dynamic balance between male and female energies in implementing and managing its social and cultural progression. In the early stages of its evolution, the social entity requires a greater ratio of male to female energy for its protection from predators and for the provision of food and shelter.

As it progresses and increases in social complexity, the need for greater feminine energy arises. Human compassion, effective interpersonal negotiations, sensitivity to multidimensional personnel requirements and rapid intuitive assessment of complicated systems all require a strong dose of feminine energy, known as the Sacred Feminine.

Arguably, the most significant damage organized religion has visited upon the world is the demise of the intuitive and creative presence and force of the Sacred Feminine. Eckhart Tolle points out that "During a three-hundred-year period between three and four million women were tortured and killed by the 'Holy Inquisition,' an institution founded by the Roman Catholic Church to suppress heresy."[82] This incomprehensible tragedy is on par with the Holocaust. In effect the Sacred Feminine was considered demonic and, as Tolle points out, an entire critical dimension was expunged from the human experience.

Although with less violence, other cultures and religions such as Judaism, Buddhism and Islam also suppressed the Sacred Feminine. The result throughout our history was that the role of women was relegated to bearing children and essentially being the "property" of men. In parts of our world, this is still the case, often with horrific outcomes.

These actions were inflicted primarily out of fear by men who sought to maintain full control of their church, their religion and the faithful. Blinded by this fear and groping for wealth and power, *they missed or more probably dismissed, the fundamental principle that successful progress in the evolution of the consciousness of humanity and the cosmos requires a delicate, dynamic and an ever-changing balance between masculine and feminine energies.*

The importance of a proper balance of feminine and masculine energies has been discussed extensively by metaphysicists. The general conclusion is summarized in the following observation from the metaphysics literature:

> "The Divine Feminine and Divine Masculine energy play critical roles in how you think, act, and behave. When both of them are merged together in a harmonious way, they allow you to understand life better. The process of merging both of these two energies eventually allows you to achieve true spiritual enlightenment and intelligence. For these reasons, balancing the Divine Feminine and Divine Masculine energy is the key to spiritual growth and ascension."[83]

This does not necessarily mean participation of an equal number of men and women at the same positions within the structure of religions, although the presence of more women in high-level positions within organized religions would certainly provide significant benefits to humanity and to the evolution of consciousness. But it does imply that both men and women innately possess some combination of both masculine and feminine energies that should be exercised in a dynamic and appropriately balanced ratio for the benefit of the *Whole*.

This male-inflicted war on the Sacred Feminine as well as the injection of layers of religious bureaucracy, misstatements and modifications of the actual teachings of early avatars such as Jesus and Buddha is what led to the birth of Gnosticism in Christianity, Zen in Buddhism, Vedanta in Hinduism, Sufism in Islam and Kabbalah in Judaism. The faithful were looking for truth and inner transformation. They wanted to "awaken," to truly touch their souls, their Personal Consciousness, and the hierarchy and control of male-made "carrot-and-stick" empires were not working for them.

Eckhart Tolle[84] in his analysis of what he terms the Collective Pain Body of humanity makes the following important observation:

> "The suppression of the feminine principle especially over the past two thousand years has enabled the ego to gain absolute supremacy in the collective human psyche. Although women have egos, of course, the ego can take root and grow more easily in the male form than in the female. This is because women are less mind-identified than men. They are more in touch with the inner body and the intelligence of the organism where the intuitive faculties originate. The female form is less rigidly encapsulated than the male, has greater openness and sensitivity toward other life-forms, and is more attuned to the natural world."

Tolle therefore concludes:

> "If the balance between male and female energies had not been destroyed in our planet, the ego's growth would have been greatly curtailed. We would not have declared war on nature, and we would not be so completely alienated from our *Being*."

Here, *Being* equates to Personal Consciousness, our very core, our Soul, our Essence.

Tolle maintains that the evolving ego in men, who are humanity's natural warriors and conquerors, perceived that it could achieve full control of our planet and nature only through its male energy, and to do so, it had to render the Sacred Feminine energy powerless. Unfortunately for all, including men, they have nearly succeeded.

Thus, we see that most cultures and religions have been created and managed by men with a strong masculine energy bias, or by men who have abandoned whatever Sacred Feminine instincts they possessed. However, most, if not all, of the global challenges we currently face require insight and implementation by a strong continuous dosage of Sacred Feminine energy—intuition, compassion, compromise, understanding, and a commitment to success of the *Whole*.

Avatars throughout history have intimately embraced the Sacred Feminine. For example, theological scholars have often noted that Mary Magdalene was considered by Jesus to be one of his most important disciples. There are assertions and learned historical analyses by theological scholars that Jesus did not die on the cross, and that he and Mary Magdalene married, had children, and traveled to India.[85]

In one such analysis by theological researcher Holger Kersten, Jesus' body, assumed by his Romans persecutors to be deceased (He was allegedly still alive.), was handed over to his followers.[86] With clandestine assistance from a sympathetic nobleman, they placed him in a tomb, where he was resuscitated and attended to. He, his mother Mary and his wife Mary Magdalene were said to have eventually made their way in secret to India. Both Jesus and his mother reportedly died and were buried there, and Mary Magdalene then made her way with her children to the south of France. The Church, on the other hand, reduced Mary Magdalene's role to little more than a penitent prostitute.

The Gnostic Gospels of Philip, Thomas and Mary Magdalene all note that the original 12 apostles were envious of, and I would even say, threatened by, the spiritual and intuitive powers of Mary Magdalene and the special status she held with Jesus. This concern was further expressed and underscored by the Early Church Fathers, who were deeply disturbed by Mary Magdalene's position.

In 595 AD, Pope Gregory the Great was so distressed by this issue that he decided, with no evidence whatsoever, that Mary Magdalene was a prostitute before being forgiven and redeemed by Jesus. She was cast deep into the dark shadows with all other historical positive allusions to the value of Sacred Feminine energy. The bible and scriptures were edited and rewritten to support these changes.

Although progress has been made, there is still little room for women and their thinking in the operations of organized religion. Their roles have been reduced to a minimum by men who, consciously or unconsciously, fear their capabilities and feminine attributes. The often unspoken rejoinder is that women are best suited to be capable wives and caring mothers. Over millennia, as the power base in our global society transitioned from organized religion to the corporate world, this bias has followed suit in that arena as well.

We must move to a greater balance between feminine and masculine energies in human culture and society if we are to create workable solutions to global threats such as nuclear proliferation, climate change, pandemics, astronomical gaps in wealth and healthcare distribution, and much more.

In the words of world-famous Jesuit priest and paleontologist Pierre Teilhard de Chardin, "The feminine is the most formidable of forces of matter."[87] The question is will we have the creative foresight, courage and compassion to make choices in this direction with a genuine concern for the future of our children, our grandchildren and beyond that? This is unambiguously the domain of the Sacred Feminine and the essence of the twelfth Universal Rule of Spiritual Physics.

RULE #12—ADDRESSING COMPLEX SOCIAL AND CULTURAL CHALLENGES REQUIRES AN APPROPRIATE DYNAMIC BALANCE BETWEEN MASCULINE AND FEMININE ENERGIES.

As social units progress and evolve, an increasing ratio of feminine to masculine energies is required. This evolution is a transition from a primary focus on protection from predators and provision for food and shelter, to intimate sensitivity to social and cultural complexities. This necessitates increased focus on human compassion, win-win negotiations, rapid intuitive assessment of complex systems and deep sensitivity to multidimensional social factors such as culture, gender, race and emotional intelligence. This is the domain of the Sacred Feminine, which is always committed to success of the Whole.

Fortunately, we are experiencing a fundamental shift of humanity towards higher levels of consciousness. As a consequence, the male-intensive ego is increasingly losing its grip on the human mind, and the Sacred Feminine is rising in importance to much greater levels in both women and men. All of humanity and nature will benefit. There is still hope for us to address the difficult global challenges before us.

Thus, it seems the ubiquitous power of love is indeed at work in our universe. As John Galsworthy, the 1932 Nobel laureate in literature astutely expressed through the character Uncle Jolyon in his novel *Indian Summer of A Forsyte*, "Love triumphs over everything! Love has no age, no limit, and no death."[88]

PART 2

USING THE 12 UNIVERSAL RULES
TO
CREATE THE LIFE YOU DREAM

*"Be still and
Know that I
Am with you."*

CHAPTER EIGHT
THE ART AND SCIENCE OF
MEDITATION[89]

"We don't exist unless we are deeply and sensually in touch with that which can be touched, but not known."[90]

—D. H. Lawrence (1885-1930), British novelist

Meditation Power

You have probably seen numerous references as to why the practice of meditation or mindfulness is helpful physically, emotionally and spiritually. There is a significant amount of experimental evidence to support this position. Over the years, the Dalai Lama has committed large numbers of frequently-meditating Buddhist monks, those with more than 10,000 hours of mindfulness practice, to scientific studies at MIT and other universities.[91] These studies have been extensive. For nearly 15 years, more than 100 monks have participated in research at more than 19 universities. Their physiological and emotional signals were monitored to determine if there were any meaningful changes.

For most of the 20th century, neuroscientists maintained that the brain structure was fixed at an early critical point in childhood. We now know that this is not true. Due to changes in behavior, the environment, neural processes, thinking and emotions, the brain can change its structure and volume by a process known as neuroplasticity.

Thus, it was not surprising that CAT scans of the monks' brains showed marked changes in behavior and structure, indicative of significant increases in physical and emotional wellbeing. In a number of experiments, meditation was shown to increase the volume of brain tissue in the prefrontal cortex, which plays a key role in attention, sensory information and internal body sensations.[92]

It also appears that frequent meditation slows the aging process. It does this by enhancing the action of an enzyme catalyst named telomerase, which maintains the length of DNA strands every time one of our cells divides. Normally, telomerase activity decreases with age and therefore DNA is not readily repaired in our chromosomes, and consequently the effects of aging follow. However, in the meditation studies, the telomerase maintained its activity and slowed the aging process.

There are even reports of individuals who have gone for years without food or water, supported only by intense practice of the meditation process.[93] Prahlad Jani, who practices meditation many hours a day, lives in India and is now 87 years old.[94] He claims he has not eaten or drank anything for 75 years. A few years ago, he was admitted to a reputable hospital for study and overseen by two senior physicians. Mr. Jani did not eat or drink anything for 15 days, and according to these physicians he subsequently tested healthier than a man half his age. A healthy human being could not last more than 12 days under these conditions.

People such as Mr. Jani maintain that in their deep meditative state, they are able to draw from the universe *prana*, the Sanskrit term for spiritual energy. If this is in fact true, perhaps there may be an analog in Spiritual Physics to Einstein's famous equation $E = mc^2$, which shows that energy and mass are interchangeable. It may be possible by a cosmic process to convert spiritual energy to mass or nutrition within these enlightened or illumined individuals.

I am not suggesting anything that drastic; but rather the use of a simple meditation or relaxation process to quiet the noise in your life and bring you into deeper contact with your Personal

Consciousness so that you can readily connect with Collective Consciousness and Cosmic Consciousness.

Finding The Gap

Let's start with the basic premises as to why meditation is an important tool for manifestation. One key challenge is that our reasoning and rational mind always tries to intervene by questioning whether something we seek to manifest into our lives is even possible. It does so through doubts, worries and the creation of numerous "rational" reasons why our intended manifestation is a long shot. These doubts are the result of many years of social and cultural hypnosis as to the way things "really are." To succeed in your manifestation, you must quiet the "logical" conscious mind and access the nonjudgmental subconscious. Meditation is the absolute perfect tool for this.

As discussed at length in Part I, we must recognize that Personal Consciousness, Collective Consciousness and Cosmic Consciousness constantly embrace and penetrate each other throughout the eternal evolving universe. Through their continuous communion, it is possible in principle and in practice to influence anyone and anything in the universe. In the stillness of deep awareness, we are all connected beings and exist within the consciousness of each other.

But, in order to do so, it is necessary to quiet the noise in our lives so that our subconscious can clear the path for our requests for manifestation. The very best means for this is meditation.

Through your meditative practice you quiet your mind, which is almost always in a continuous conversation with itself. Your mind is conditioned by your past history as well as by the mind-set you inherited from your parents and other forces in your life.

An exercise that can help you become increasingly more effective at meditation is to take notice as often as possible of the rambling conversations of your chatting mind. In doing this, you not only become aware of the thoughts your mind is having, but more importantly, you become aware of you as the witness to these thoughts. That "you," which is felt as a pleasant still presence, is the real *you*. It's your true *Self*, your soul, your Personal Consciousness, your Atman, through which you are experiencing an enhanced and deeper dimension of consciousness.

At this point, because you are observing the thought, you de-energize the mind and most particularly the ego, and the thought dissipates. You become more alert and fully present. Also, and this is key, when the thought subsides, you will experience what is called a "gap" in your thinking—the complete absence of thought. For some brief period you have no thoughts; your mind is blank. This stillness and peace you experience will with time and practice bring you closer to *Oneness* with your inner *Self,* indeed your Personal Consciousness or soul.

These gaps are a source of joy and fulfillment, and are responsible for creative strokes of genius. *Einstein, da Vinci and many other accomplished artists and inventors often said that their most creative insights came not when they were thinking about a problem, but in a moment of intense silence—the gap.* The reason for this is that they likely previously wrestled with the idea or question and at the time saw no solution or insight.

However, the answer and insight is always known by Personal Consciousness because it is completely embraced by Cosmic Consciousness, which is Universal Intelligence. It knows all. To hear it clearly, what is often called an "aha moment," it is necessary to quiet the normal mental noise we all experience. Meditation does just that.

You can foster the creation of these gaps of non-mindedness by staying completely focused on what you are doing. If you are washing the dishes, think about every step—scraping the plates, running the water, adding and mixing the soap; or neatly placing the dishes in the dishwasher. In this mode, your thinking is highly focused on the task at hand, and your mind does not experience its normal chaotic chatter. As Eckhart Tolle would surely say, "You are experiencing the Power of NOW."

In time, you will find that two things happen. First, there is an increase in the level of deep peace you feel within your spirit, and second, it will be much easier to enter a state of relaxation or meditation.

Then as you proceed, your mind will experience an increasing number of gaps and for longer periods of time. Each time you create one of these gaps in your mind you increase your ability to access and use the potential and knowledge of your Personal Consciousness.

No Magic

There is no magic to meditation. It requires practice and consistency; however, it is true that people vary in their innate ability to meditate. The most frequent reason they give up on meditation is that when they first begin they find that it is quite difficult to quiet their mind to a single thought or mantra, what is known as single-pointed concentration. This is completely normal. In fact, even for frequent practitioners, these challenges can occur. It is simply a kind of cleansing of the mind, getting rid of subconscious "junk" from your Personal Consciousness.

Sometimes you may even dredge up thoughts that you consider improper, inappropriate, or disturbing. This is normal, especially as you begin to learn to meditate. You are basically doing some house-cleaning of your subconscious, which for many years may have stored thoughts and memories that no longer serve you well. It is best to be patient and benefit from this cleansing.

It is only necessary to do two things when this happens; let it not bother you in any way; and simply observe and then release the unwanted thoughts and return to your single focus—no matter how often this occurs. It is important not to judge your thoughts; just look at them and let them go. Dismissing mental interruptions gets easier with time and trying, and the eventual benefits are worth your effort.

Mantras

In any relaxation or meditation process, it is beneficial to use a mantra, a word or words that help you focus your mind on a spiritual person, place or thing. Below I provide a list of frequently used mantras. They are all in the Sanskrit language, where often a few words have a much longer translation into English to provide the appropriate essence or meaning.

The value of Sanskrit is that as an ancient foreign language, these mantras do not readily elicit extraneous thoughts the way words well-known in our own vocabulary might. That being said, it is certainly true that many people do meditate on the names and images of saints and avatars such as Buddha, Jesus, Krishna and others.

There is also the practice of Transcendental Meditation (TM). Usually this is learned at a TM center and at the end of the course, your teacher provides you with a Sanskrit mantra, a word that has essentially no meaning, so that you are not distracted by it. You are instructed that this is your mantra for life and that you are never to disclose it to anyone. The key in meditation is to do what works best for you. There is no magic.

Here are some mantras that you might consider, along with a loose translation of their meanings:

Om—A reflection of the Absolute Reality—Cosmic Consciousness or God.

I Am—Alternate name for Cosmic Consciousness or God; sometimes used as "I am I AM," which translates to "I am God." Or God is within me, which reflects one of the 12 Universal Rules.

Aham Brahmasmi—The core of my being is the ultimate reality, the root of the universe, the source of all that exists.

Sat, Chit, Ananda—Existence, consciousness, bliss.

Ram, Ram, Ram—Everything I desire is within me.

Om, Bhavnam Namah—I am absolute existence. I am a field of all possibilities.

Om, Vardhanam Namah—I nourish the universe, and the universe nourishes me.

Om Kriyam Namah—My actions are aligned with cosmic law.

Om Anandham Namah—My actions are free from attachments to the outcome.

Generally, it is advisable to get comfortable with one mantra and use it exclusively. Over time, it will become your close spiritual friend and be helpful to quickly eliciting a sense of calm.

Relaxation

As a pre-step to meditation, it is helpful to achieve a level of deep relaxation. According to *Raja Yoga*, developed in India a few thousand years ago, the spinal column contains two primary nerve currents—the *Ida* path on the left of the column and the *Pingala* path on the right. There is also a central passageway within the spinal column called *Sushumna*. The two nerve current pathways are important for facilitating movement through the Sushumna passageway of the *kundalini*, which according to Raja Yoga physiology is a huge reserve of consciousness energy, situated at the base of the spine.

In Sanskrit, kundalini means "coiled up." This energy is difficult to arouse and takes much practice to do so. However, according to Hindu wisdom, when it is aroused and released, it is said to travel up the spine through what are known as the six centers or lotuses of consciousness, reaching the seventh center, located at the core of your brain. As the kundalini energy reaches higher centers, it produces increasing degrees of enlightenment—the seventh level inducing intense bliss, which is experienced usually only by those well practiced in relaxation and meditation techniques.

There are advanced breathing procedures called *Pranayama*, which are designed to arouse and expeditiously release the kundalini energy; however, in the hands of uninformed or unpracticed individuals, these procedures can be very dangerous. Used improperly, they can cause physical and mental impairment and worse. I won't describe them here as they are too risky to practice and are not necessary at all for our needs.

However, I would like to outline a few breathing techniques as they are beneficial not only for relaxation, but also for your long-term health and vitality. Eastern Wisdom teaches that these simple breathing procedures can not only prevent and heal disease, but also when practiced daily, they can extend your life span.

This may not come as a surprise when you consider that the air cells in your lungs, known as alveoli, if spread out on a flat surface, make up an area of more than 1,500 square meters and oxygenate more than 17,000 liters of your blood every 24 hours.

Eastern Traditions maintain that not only does efficient oxygenation of your blood have huge health benefits, but they note that inhalation also ingests into your body the life-giving force *prana*. It is this force, when properly infused into the body, that reportedly has enabled numerous so-called yogis to live without sleep, food, and in some instances, water, for extended periods of time. These yogis also maintain that prana is the source of their ability to cure others of disease through a process known as magnetic healing.

For our purposes, I will present two simple, yet powerful breathing techniques for relaxation and improved health and vitality: Complete Breathing and Cleansing Breathing.[95]

Complete Breathing

The following technique is outlined in several distinct steps. However, once learned, it is best carried out in one smooth process. It is a powerful means to increased vitality, relaxation and stress reduction.

❖ Stand erect, breathing only through your nostrils.

❖ Breathe slowly into your lower lungs by extending your diaphragm (belly). This is exactly how newborns breathe. We unfortunately unlearn this technique as we get older.

❖ Continue your inhalation by breathing into the middle section of your lungs, pushing out your lower ribs and breast bone.

❖ Complete your breath by breathing into your upper lungs, protruding your upper chest and lifting your upper ribs. I find it helpful to lift the shoulders slightly in this step.

❖ Final movement—The lower part of your abdomen is drawn in slightly, which gives some support to your lungs and also helps fill any remaining space in your upper lungs.

❖ Retain your breath for 5 seconds.

❖ Finally, exhale slowly, maintaining your chest in a firm position and lifting upwards slowly as the air leaves your lungs.

❖ It is helpful to practice this, bare-chested in front of a mirror and note the movements of your abdomen and chest.

Cleansing Breathing

This breathing technique will not only have the same results as Complete Breathing, but it also detoxifies the body and is an excellent "recharging" mechanism for when you are tired. Again, detailed steps are described, but after some practice all steps are best carried out in one smooth motion.

❖ Carry out one round of Complete Breathing.

❖ After the 5-second retention step, exhale all remaining air in the following manner.

  ▪ Pucker your lips as if to whistle, but do not swell your cheeks.

  ▪ With relatively intense vigor, exhale a small amount of air through your lips.

  ▪ Stop after a slight exhale.

  ▪ Repeat another small exhale and then stop again.

❖ Repeat this procedure until all air is exhaled.

If you prefer simplicity, there is a well-known procedure that is most helpful in achieving relaxation quite quickly. It involves only modest arousal of the kundalini energy and can be easily and safely practiced by anyone as follows:

❖ Find a quiet place where you will not be disturbed by anyone or anything. Sit comfortably in the lotus position, or if that is uncomfortable, use a chair with a rigid back support. It is fine to lean back, however the spine and neck must remain erect even though you are in a relaxed position.

❖ To help induce a state of relaxation, close your eyes and create a picture in your mind that you consider to be of striking beauty. Perhaps, it's a seaside vista or any number of places you have experienced in your past. Pictures of beauty are powerful catalysts for creating a deep state of relaxation.

❖ Close your eyes and depress the right nostril with the thumb of your right hand and breathe in deeply through your left nostril. Try to do this slowly and smoothly over a period of about 10 seconds. As you inhale focus on the air you are inhaling as containing pure conscious energy (prana). Envision it as a life-breath sending a current of energy down the Ida nerve bundle to your kundalini situated in a triangular lotus at the base of your spine.

❖ Hold your breath for about 10 seconds, mentally repeating your mantra, if you have one. If not, use the universal sacred mantra, OM, or any of the others I have listed above. During this third period allow the prana to stimulate the kundalini.

❖ As you release the right nostril, close the left nostril with your forefinger and over 10 seconds slowly exhale the air in your lungs through your right nostril, envisioning as you do so that you are expelling negative energy and conscious impurities from your body. You might even envision smoke emitting from your nostril, thereby allowing your body, mind and consciousness to achieve a cleaner state of being.

❖ Keeping your left nostril closed, now inhale slowly over 10 seconds through the right nostril, filling your lungs to capacity and sending a current of prana energy down the pingala nerve bundle adjacent to your spine directly to the kundalini and stimulate it as before.

❖ Continue this process for 10 minutes, alternating nostril closures. This technique is safe to practice and is known to moderately stimulate the energy situated at the base of your spine. It is a helpful tool for relaxation and preparation for your meditation.

An alternate very simple procedure is the following:

❖ With your eyes closed, breathe in deeply through both nostrils for 5 seconds and hold your breath for another 5 seconds.

❖ Then breathe out for 20 seconds through narrowly-pursed lips (do not puff your cheeks), as though you were slowly blowing out candles on a birthday cake.

❖ Repeat this 10 times.

A number of people I know, including me on occasion, use the smoke and fumes from smoldering frankincense as a relaxation facilitator. It is a legal material and can be purchased on-line or at most religious supply stores. It is available in the form of small rocks or *tears* of frankincense resin, and can be melted and volatilized on a charcoal briquette in a small ceramic or metal container. It has been used for millennia as a means to facilitate mental clarity, stress reduction and overall centeredness.

Meditation

If you are interested in becoming a serious practitioner of meditation, you may want to take a course. Alternatively, you can find any number of books which explain the practice, purpose and physiological effects of meditation. However, a simple yet effective means to meditate is as follows:

❖ Practice one of the above-described relaxation techniques for 10 minutes.

❖ Continue to sit in the same lotus position, or on a chair, maintaining your eyes closed and your spine erect.

❖ Bring your mental focus to your heart—not your biological heart, but the center of your chest, just to the right and adjacent to your physical heart. Breathe normally.

❖ Imagine a bright white light source coming from a distance into your heart.

❖ It is also helpful, although not necessary, to focus your mind on your mantra while you have this vision. If you have no mantra at this time, use the universal sacred mantra, OM, or one of the mantras I have listed earlier.

❖ In the beginning and even periodically after you have practiced meditation for some time, your focus will be broken by mundane thoughts, very much so as you experience all of the time. "What is my schedule today?" "I wonder if Bob will be at work today." "Gee, I would love to try that new Chinese restaurant." This mental chatter is normal, especially when you first begin to practice meditation. The most important thing is to NOT let it bother you. Simply and casually regain your focus on your mantra. In the Eastern Wisdom Traditions, these thoughts are said to result from *Samskaras* ("impression" in Sanskrit), imprints on your mind, which must be released to achieve consistent and constant focus on the NOW.

❖ In the beginning, meditate for about 20 minutes. After a few weeks, increase to 30 minutes, and after a few more weeks, increase to 40 minutes. That is sufficient. However, even 20 minutes per day, preferably in the early morning, is sufficient to have significant benefits.

❖ I find the following regimen very effective. Rise early, say at 5:30 a.m. Use the bathroom and shower, preparing for your day. Next do 10 minutes of stretching exercises to energize your mind and body. Then proceed to relaxation and meditation.

❖ To the extent that it is practical, practice your relaxation and meditation techniques in the same place and at the same time each day.

❖ A variation of this technique is to practice relaxation in the evening before going to sleep and meditation in the morning. Both of these approaches, if practiced faithfully and carefully, can bring excellent results. Meditation is best done when all others are either asleep or in a separate part of the home.

If you become discouraged because it's taking too long for you to reach a deep state of meditation, don't give up. One thing you might try instead is to use only one of the above-described relaxation techniques. It's easy to do and eventually you will move naturally into the art of meditation.

Go to the gap; it will change your life, forever.

"Dream ...
Imagine ...
Believe ...
Manifest ..."

CHAPTER NINE
CREATING YOUR DREAMS

"Fools exploit the world; the wise transfigure it. It is the highest wisdom to know that in the living universe there is no destiny other than that created out of imagination of man. There is no influence outside of the mind of man"[96]

Neville Goddard (1905-72), Spiritual Teacher

Most people are completely unaware of the fundamental *Law of Creation—you and only you create each and every outcome you experience in life with your five senses.*[97] How is this apparent miraculous process possible—possible for anyone and everyone? If it's truly possible, are there important guidelines that you must follow to successfully manifest into your life those things you desire? Let's look at the answer to these two questions. We can answer the first by examining the domain where quantum physics overlaps with the emerging field of Spiritual Physics. To do this we must draw on a few important findings discussed in Part I.

The Discontinuity

According to Universal Rules 4 and 5, the real world is not what we perceive with our five senses. The universe and everything in it came about by arising simultaneously in the field of infinite and eternal Cosmic Consciousness, which intimately embraces your Personal Consciousness and Collective Consciousness. This means consciousness is our complete ground of being, our true reality, and by our conscious observation we create the limited physical reality we perceive with our five senses. Your five-sense perceived reality is best considered an illusion and certainly not your true reality.

Quantum physics tells us that even though the world appears to our five senses as pictures, sounds, tastes, fragrances and textures, in "true reality," this is not the case. Australian biologist and Nobel laureate John Carew Eccles was fond of saying, "There are no colors in the real world; there are no textures in the real world; there are no fragrances in the real world; what actually exists out there is some radically ambiguous and ceaselessly flowing quantum soup."[98] The magic is in our consciousness, because out of that milieu we evoke in our consciousness a physical world, the entire universe. How does this come about? How does this apparent mystical phenomenon occur and how can it be used to change your physical "illusionary" world for the better? How can you expeditiously manifest into your life those things that will bring you long-term happiness and fulfillment?

Everything in the universe before conscious observation is not solid mass; it consists of an infinite number of vibrations, that is to say a continuous, rapid, circuitous switching of energy waves between the states of "on" and "off." Physicists call this a *discontinuity*, a point at which a signal abruptly and instantly undergoes change, such as continuously switching a light bulb between the on and off positions. This is in distinct contrast to a continuous and gradual change such as driving your car up a smooth, modestly increasing hill until the incline slowly levels out to a flat plane.

The on-off switch is a good metaphor for the generation of our five-sense reality. For example, when you look at a neon sign creating a complex apparently moving picture or an advertisement message, there really is no moving picture or message. It is simply a large number of neon lamps perfectly timed to switch on and off so that an illusion of a moving picture or written message is created.

Similarly, what we call the physical world is not its real essence, despite what we perceive with our five senses. It is in reality a discontinuity, an on-off signal that gives us the experience of the world and the universe and everything in it.

"Ah, but," you say, "I am a solid composite of flesh and bones, and when I see you and shake your hand, we both experience the solidity of a person!" This is an illusion. First of all, it is our mutual observation (the *Observation Effect*) that "materializes" each of us from a vibrating energy field to what appears to be what we define as a person. You and I are a pile of some 40 trillion cells or 260 trillion-trillion atoms, stacked together and connected in a manner consistent with the connecting or so-called bonding rules of chemistry for various atoms and molecules.

Atoms and molecules are not solid at all. They are entities composed only of energy and information. The reason you experience solidity when you shake my hand is due to a law of quantum physics known as the *Pauli Exclusion Principle*. It states that only a discrete and specifically defined number of electrons are allowed at any one time in a given place, more accurately, within a specific energy level.

So when you shake my hand, electrons rapidly transgressing the atoms that make up my hand are pushed back and excluded from intermingling with the electrons in your hand. It's the same reason we don't sink into the earth, or the floor we walk on. This quantum mechanical pushing force makes both of us seem as though we are solid. But we are not. We are essentially empty space filled with energy and information, and we are vibrating at certain frequencies until we observe each other. At that instant, my vibrating energy field collapses (*decoherence*) to what you "see," and similarly for me when I encounter you. We, of course, also materialize ourselves by self observation with one or more of our five senses.

There are five attributes of the discontinuity that are important for understanding how your ability to manifest or create something within your life can come about in practice.

Composition is the first attribute of the discontinuity. In the "on" position, the content of the discontinuity is energy and information. The energy (E) contained in any material object, by Einstein's famous formula $E = mc^2$, is equivalent to the mass of the object multiplied by the square of the speed of light. This means that the physical presence of anything, that is to say its mass (m), can be created from energy present in the discontinuity. Information is infinite knowledge, namely, all that is known and necessary for manifestation at any time past, present and future. It is omniscience, a key attribute of Cosmic Consciousness.

In the "off" position, there exists no energy, mass or material objects, only vibrating probability waves which are orchestrated and managed by Cosmic Consciousness. These waves are describable by the laws of modern quantum physics as an infinite number of possibility waves. They can in principle be represented by the famous Schrödinger wave equation and describe an infinite number of possible outcomes. It is what Nobel laureate Werner Heisenberg, one of the fathers of quantum physics, called the realm of "potentia," the immeasurable potential for all that was, all that is, and all that will or could ever be. The on-off signal between these two states of the discontinuity provides us with our five-sense experience of the world.

Non-local Correlation is the second attribute of the discontinuity. This means that everything in the entire universe is synchronized, correlated, in harmony and coincidental with everything else. This correlation occurs instantly, faster than the speed of light, or as physicists like to say, superluminally.

This instantaneous phenomenon occurs across space-time, where past, present, future and distance in all of space are connected instantly and eternally. Time does not exist in the realm of consciousness. It is a man-made fabrication necessary to manage our lives without chaos. In fact, we can say that as we view and define time, all creation that ever occurred or ever will occur, is present in the eternal now. Yes, creation is complete. This point is summarized so well by Neville Goddard:[99]

"Creation is complete. Creativeness is only a deeper receptiveness, for the entire contents of all time and all space. While experienced in a time sequence, all creation actually coexists in an infinite and eternal now. In other words, all that you ever have been or ever will be—in fact all that mankind ever was or ever will be exits now. This is what is meant by creation, and the statement that creation is finished means nothing is ever to be created, it is only to be manifested. What is called creativeness is only becoming aware of what already is."

In my view, creativity is the unique ability through the power of Personal Consciousness, your soul, to choose a single outcome among all of the possibilities for a given event, and then manifest it into your life as desired.

Non-local correlation occurs even though there appears to be no force field between objects. This non-local correlation effect is responsible for what we call simultaneity in the universe, and especially in managing the precise and healthy functioning of all biological organisms. In Chapter 1, we discussed The Great Cosmic Connection in the context of your 40 trillion cells instantly communicating for the good of the Whole, namely, you and everything in our universe.

Heisenberg's Uncertainty Principle is the third attribute of the discontinuity. It states that it is impossible to know precisely both the energy and position of anything. If you knew the exact location of an electron, its energy would be infinite. If you knew its precise energy, its location would be spread out over infinity.

By this principle, we cannot know precisely if and when a given event or manifestation will occur. We can only know the probability of its occurrence. If the wave equation for a desired outcome within the realm of the potentia is represented by ψ, then ψ^2 that is to say the square of ψ is directly proportional to the probability of the desired manifestation occurring. This was originally figured out by Nobel laureate physicist Max Born, another of the great names in the foundations of quantum physics.

The probability of manifestation or creation can be increased significantly by a specific process invoking the information contained in the discontinuity, namely, Cosmic Consciousness. For all intents and purposes, you can increase the probability of a manifestation occurring and therefore essentially create near certainty for a desired outcome.

Quantum Creativity is the fourth attribute of the discontinuity. It is what Deepak Chopra refers to as a creativity wherein patterns of intelligence, information and energy move from one expression or point in existence to a completely new one with no transitional phase. In its simplest form it is like moving from here to there without any presence or existence in between. This happens in the quantum world all the time. For example, within the atoms which make up your body, electrons are often moving from one energy level to another. In this process, an electron disappears from for example a high energy level and jumps down to a lower energy level, it does not exist in-between these levels.

This is known as a "quantum jump." This kind of quantum phenomenon where something happens at one point, causing something to happen at another point with no presence in between was referred to by Einstein as "spooky action at a distance."[100] Although he was very much bothered by it, in many years of research, he was unable to find a means to justify or refute it. Perhaps the reason for his lack of success is that although there is some overlap between quantum physics and Spiritual Physics, the laws of the latter are very different and currently not completely known.

This quantum creativity is not unlike the popular science fiction show, Star Trek, where Captain Kirk enters the base of the Starship Enterprise and says, "Beam me up Scotty." Scotty pushes a button, and the captain disappears from the base only to show up at the captain's deck, and he never appears in-between. Some metaphysicists believe that this may be the mechanism for reincarnation and the Karmic Law, namely the means whereby patterns of intelligence, information and energy move from one person to another subsequent to the death of the former and the birth of the latter.

Observer Effect is the fifth attribute of the discontinuity. Suffice it to say at this point that as physicist and cosmologist, the late John Archibald Wheeler noted, "The physical universe would not exist if there were not conscious beings looking at it."[101] As incomprehensible as it may be, even to physicists, unless there is a conscious being looking at the universe, it remains a vibration, a discontinuity of infinite potentia waves.

This means that the universe is in constant energetic vibration of a nearly infinite number of quantum waves rapidly switching on and off. It requires a conscious being to observe the discontinuity and thereby collapse it and somehow convert it into sound, taste, color, form, smell, what we call the physical universe.

These five characteristics of the discontinuity support the conclusion that the discontinuity is a pure manifestation of Cosmic Consciousness. It is an intimate part of your spirit or soul; it is your Personal Consciousness if you like, which is eternal and infinite and completely enmeshed with the fabric of Cosmic Consciousness.

Your soul is not just a "thing." It is a field of infinite possibilities. Your soul embraces uncertainty because the greater the level of uncertainty, the greater the level of creativity—when something is completely known, there is zero possibility for creativity. And as such, your soul is the omnipresent, omniscient, omnipotent awareness that as you read this very sentence is orchestrating with simultaneity the hundreds of trillions of things that are happening in your body. *Your soul (Personal Consciousness) co-creates with God (Cosmic Consciousness) all that you experience in your five-sense world, which is why you can manifest your dreams should you desire to do so.*

Let's now explore the answer to the second question, "Are there important guidelines that you must follow to successfully manifest those things you seek and desire to create the life that you dream?"

The Law of Manifestation

There have been numerous self-help books written on The Law of Manifestation or the Law of Attraction to create what you desire in life. In my experience, a positive attitude and expectation can be most valuable in the process. However, to be consistently effective in the manifestation process requires a series of steps, each important to achieve the end result in a timely and efficient manner. These steps have been developed over millennia by spiritually-adept wisdom seekers, and have proven to work for thousands, if not millions of people.

The experientially-proven premise of this process is that all of creation is already done. Everything you could possibly want is accessible to you by going inside to your Personal Consciousness, not outside. The connectivity between your Personal Consciousness, Collective Consciousness and Cosmic Consciousness is eternally present. To manifest your dreams, you just need to use the appropriate program to access this incredible asset, which deep down you already possess.

There are five steps to manifest, with the least amount of effort, those physical and spiritual elements you seek to be an intimate part of your life. Although some of these steps are more challenging than others, all are equally important for manifestation. They are *Attention, Intention, Imagination, Belief* and *Detachment*. With practice, each of these steps can be carried out in a seamless path that requires minimal energy on your part, and always leads to success. With practice, the time to manifestation will become shorter and shorter to a point where the process can in some circumstances be achieved almost instantaneously. There are two prerequisites for this process to proceed smoothly.

First, the desired outcome must be beneficial to you and indirectly, if not directly, to others (benefits the *Whole*). At a minimum, there can be no negative impact on the evolution of Cosmic Consciousness. There have been instances where this technique has been used at the borderline between benefit and disadvantage of Cosmic Consciousness, and subsequently the manifestor subsequently slipped into a negative spiral. In such cases of greed or self-centeredness, ignoble actions inevitably result in unhappy consequences to the "manifestor." What goes around comes around. It's part of the universal fabric of Karma.

Second, these five steps are most effectively achieved through a deep connection with your Personal Consciousness. Beyond being born an avatar, the only known means for human beings to achieve this deep connection is through some form of meditation.

In meditation, you access the spiritual realm of consciousness and the interconnectivity of Personal Consciousness, Collective Consciousness and Cosmic Consciousness. This enables you to control your beliefs, expectations and intentions so that you can effortlessly access the unlimited abundance available through the universe of consciousness. This process is necessary for most of us because as psychiatrist Carl Jung noted many years ago, most of our beliefs are based on what others have taught us—our parents, teachers, friends or the media. Jung called this the great *Collective Consciousness*, not to be confused with the same term used in this book.

If any of these beliefs would interfere with achieving your goals, they must be erased or reprogrammed to support your endeavor. Although some of this potentially detrimental information resides within our consciousness, most of it is deeply buried in our subconscious. Fortunately, as conscious human beings, we have the amazing ability to change any past conditioning and reprogram our subconscious. The means for this is meditation.

The reason that people sometimes fail to achieve their desired goals by simply practicing positive thinking or various forms of The

Law of Attraction is that these methods often do not explain the power and potential of each of the five specific steps and the necessity to meet the two prerequisites mentioned above. People who fail to manifest their intended objective often rationalize this outcome by saying, "I must have done something incorrectly." And they are correct.

It is also important to focus on a single manifestation at a time, and not to have a "laundry list" of desires in a single meditation sitting. So, it is best to prioritize your goals and work on one at a time. It is important to be as specific as possible and to create vivid, detailed, mental pictures during the process. This will fire up your imagination, your passion and your belief in success of the manifestation.

Let's see how these five steps mesh together for successful manifestation of your personal desires.

Attention—This is the first step in any personal transformation, and it always starts with a thought. Let's say you are concerned about your health and you turn your attention to what you might do to improve it. You contemplate a number of actions that could address this issue such as: get an annual physical exam; create a practical exercise regime; modify your diet to include only healthy foods; and consider a vacation that is more active physically than your usual respites. You begin to feel the excitement about the potential and development of your plan. Placing your attention on this area begins to expand a number of possibilities into your life, often ones that you may not have conceived of previously.

Attention on a specific issue of prime interest creates the early stages of intense passion, and is a source of emotional and physical energy. Placing your attention on exactly what you want in your world, whether it is love, prosperity, a job, improved health or anything else that meets the requisite criteria, will energize that object, the individuals associated with it, and as a consequence begin to draw it to you. It does this by initiating the process of connecting and communicating more intimately with your Personal Consciousness and the Collective Consciousness of the world around you. This connection will grow stronger as you proceed through the remaining four steps of manifestation.

Intention—Intention is an absolutely crystal-clear specific vision of a desired outcome. Your intention starts with a thought, a clear understanding of something you would like to have happen. You must believe that you can attain your goal, as long as it brings no harm to anyone or anything.

In this step, consider something that you would like to change or perhaps to manifest into your life. Then focus all of your thoughts on this intention. It is useful to write down your intention and in doing so it is best to be as specific as possible. Adjectives of clarification and description are most helpful such as, "I currently weigh 70 kilograms (154 pounds). I will weigh 60 kilograms (132 pounds)," or simply, "I will weigh 60 kilograms."

The next step is to enter into meditation as described in Chapter 8. At some point, when you have achieved deep serenity, open your eyes and read your intention. Then close your eyes again and in your mind's eye surrender your intention to the universe, and let the universe decide on the details of when and how to achieve your goal. Just as attention energizes you towards your goal, intention will begin the process of the necessary transformations required to achieve your goal. It strengthens the intimacy and unity among Personal Consciousness, Collective Consciousness and Cosmic Consciousness. They are the forces that will fulfill your desires.

What may emerge is something like: "I will go to the fitness center on Monday, Wednesday and Friday and do a specific exercise regime, preceded and followed by specific stretching exercises. My diet will consist mainly of approximately 150 gram (5 ½ ounces) portions of chicken or fish and two servings of green vegetables; no deserts and no alcohol." You are well on your way to using your consciousness to manifest your dreams. Notice the necessity for details.

To summarize and emphasize, there are three aspects of consciousness that you are tapping into: Soul (Personal Consciousness), Matter (Collective Consciousness) and Spirit (Cosmic Consciousness). Your Personal Consciousness creates the goals that you seek to achieve and assures that they are in the best interest of you and the *Whole.* You connect with Collective Consciousness for any assistance you will need from others. And Cosmic Consciousness creates the specific recipe for your success and sees that it is transmitted to and orchestrated within the realms of Personal Consciousness and Collective Consciousness. You don't have to worry about details of implementation; they are all handled by the universe. In fact, it could be detrimental for you to do so.

Imagination—Imagination is the next key step in the manifestation process. It is also one of the most powerful forces in human consciousness. You must imagine what you desire; and ultimately you must believe it to be true for it to be manifested into your life. This means that in moments of quiet relaxation, you can envision pictures in your mind of what you seek to achieve or to manifest into your life. The purpose of imagination is to transition you to the next step which is belief. Using our earlier example, picture yourself with the healthy physique and high energy level you aspire to!

I love the words of the great English poet William Blake concerning his thoughts on imagination. In his magical poem, Jerusalem, he writes "I rest not from my great task to open the Eternal Worlds, to open the immortal Eyes of Man inwards into the Worlds of Thought: into Eternity ever expanding in the Bosom of God, the Human Imagination."

The important means to imagination are not simply words in your mind. You need pictures, detailed pictures which create feelings. Persistence is the key. This is also the approach taken by most successful athletes in a process they call sport visualization. They picture their success before it happens.

You can experience feeling of natural about achieving your objective through persistently filling your Personal Consciousness with detailed imagination; for example, picture yourself being what you want to be, or having what you desire. This method speaks to your subconscious, which is not a judge and takes everything you tell it as fact as long as you don't erase these desired facts with hesitation and doubt. And if you are bothered by doubt, have no fear, persist and eventually all doubt and hesitation will evaporate.

In this process you must keep in mind that you have infinite freewill to choose your assumptions, but absolutely no power or means to determine the conditions, timing and events that will lead to your goal or objective. You must leave those details to the universe, more specifically, to Cosmic Consciousness which will work this process through the presence of Collective Consciousness. This is an aspect of Spiritual Physics we have yet to understand with any depth.

We know from vast experience that everyone and anyone can achieve their goals and objectives if they follow the path I am describing here. We know that all are entitled to the very best under these circumstances. We know that Cosmic Consciousness is the great Universal Intelligence and Orchestrator, and we know that all of the necessary physical, emotional and spiritual needs are available through the auspices of our Collective Consciousness connection. However, we don't yet understand how Cosmic Consciousness directs Collective Consciousness and the interaction with your Personal Consciousness to manifest your desires. This is one aspect of Spiritual Physics yet to be uncovered.

The best means to practice the assumption of success is to consistently support your desire for your objective. This begins with intention, grows with attention and intensifies with imagination. Now you must learn how to use the power of minimum distraction through the practice of physical immobility. This can be accomplished while lying in bed in the evening, just before going to sleep, or even better when you are just awakening in the morning. Your semi-conscious mental state will be one similar to sleep, but one in which you can control the subject and focus of your attention.

At this point you are not distracted by your physical movements, or those around you. Remaining still as you lie in bed, you will be able to develop the strong mental force that this stillness brings forth. This altered state of awareness is closely related to subconsciously-induced hypnosis. It will enable you to significantly increase your power of concentration.

Take several deep breaths and continue to quiet your mind as you would in meditation. In your serene relaxation reverie, you can then begin to assume that your wish is already fulfilled. Your conscious judging or reasoning mind will likely retaliate with logical counter arguments; however, by this time you are probably experiencing your focused intention to realize your endpoint, your goal. As you begin to think from the endpoint, you may struggle to feel the intense sensation of the accomplishment of your objective. It is best to do this exercise daily, preferably each morning upon awakening. You are now ready to enter the next step—belief.

Belief—*It's not what you want that you attract into your life; it's what you believe to be true.* The only way that I know for you to make the transition from imagination to belief is to feel the intense pleasure of having accomplished your goal. You must revel in your success. It's here already and it feels great.

The time that is required for you to achieve your objective is directly proportional to the naturalness and authenticity of your feelings of having already achieved it. Not feeling natural is a sure direction to failure. You can have a deep desire, strong intention, and faithfully follow the steps described here, but if you do not feel absolutely natural in your objective, and mentally celebrate your accomplishment, it cannot easily come about in a timely manner. However, tenacity and persistence in practice always overcomes doubt and hesitation. So don't give up.

If it does not feel natural to you to get the promotion you seek, you will not get it. This is why we precede belief with assumption because we find that persistent assumption eventually leads to belief. In the words of Neville Goddard, "Assume the feeling of your wish fulfilled and continue feeling that it is fulfilled until that which you feel objectifies itself. If a physical fact can produce a psychological state, a psychological state can produce a physical fact." They are reversible.

He goes on to underscore that "When the power of belief and will are in conflict, belief invariably wins."[102] When the thought "I believe" becomes very strong in an altered state of consciousness, it transitions to the most powerful possible powerful assertion—"I know."

As a closing of anticipated gratitude and personal endorsement to the success of your manifestation, I suggest that you mentally, and even better, verbally, close with the exclamation: "It is done!" or "So be it!" or simply, "Amen!"

Detachment—Now for the last and arguably the most difficult step—detachment. So let's spend some time gaining insight into this.

I have purposely used the word "detachment" and not "unattachment," which is sometimes used in other texts on manifestation. I believe the latter signifies that throughout the process you were never attached to the goal you seek to manifest, while detachment means, as is normally the case, you are attached to your goal and now must make an effort to relinquish your attachment. I believe this is a more accurate assessment of the reality of the process.

You might argue, "I have done all the work necessary to get this far, and now you want me to detach from the outcome?" Yes, and the reason is quite simple. If you don't detach from the desired outcome of achieving your goal or objective, your logical mind can very easily fall back on the fear of failure. And fear is the great negative attractor.

You always attract what your fear, and that which you fear the most, comes swiftly to your doorstep. The reason that you fail when you fear is the very same reason you succeed when you assume that a desired outcome has already happened. Fear induces all of the physical, emotional, spiritual and psychological feelings you need for a negative manifestation. Fear is a powerful paralyzing force. It has the ability to rapidly move through all five stages of the manifestation process.

In my opinion, there is only one counter force that can completely erase the presence of fear, or help you make any critical change for that matter. It's the energy of unbridled passion. This creative force is so powerful that it evaporates fear from the deepest level of the human spirit and can literally change the world. It has done so many times before.

Think back in your own life to when you achieved a significant accomplishment; perhaps, a sports medal, or a college degree, or an award for some achievement; or perhaps it was reaching a goal you set for yourself concerning fitness or academic excellence. Almost certainly this required an intense level of passion and the more difficult the challenge, the more passion it required, ultimately yielding a deep sense of fulfillment.

This kind of passion enabled many innovators to change the world. Leonardo da Vinci, Rachel Carson, Isaac Newton, Marie Curie, Thomas Edison, Maria Montessori, Albert Einstein, Jonas Salk, and thousands of lesser known change-makers, all left their indelible imprint on humanity. Each of them discovered their personal capability or Essence and connected it with an important need in the world. In doing so they were driven by a personal vision that ignited their passion, and that spark ultimately became a flame, which in turn became a torch, and it changed the world through the power of innovation.[103] Unbridled passion is like that. No barrier is too high.

The mechanism by which this occurs is always the same. For these innovators, the *attention-intention-imagination-belief-detachment* process worked perfectly and their passion was so deep that the end points of belief and detachment were a foregone conclusion. Their belief was so deep and the internal picture that permeated their Personal Consciousness was so conclusive that they did not simply overcome fear with courage; but rather they achieved a state of "fearlessness." In such a state you neither concern yourself with the success or the failure of your manifestation. It just is. It exists. It's called detachment.

In this final step in the manifestation process, you must detach all of your expectations for the outcome and allow everyone and everything the complete freedom to be exactly as they are. In doing so, you achieve a state of fearlessness. You accept all uncertainty, which is the birthplace of creativity. Great uncertainty equates to high creativity, and that is what you need to enable the unlimited, abundant universe to do its job. You relinquish all desires to manage circumstances to create a specific path to your goal and its timing. Leave the details to the universe.

At this point, if you have done well in the first five steps of this process, you can have complete faith that Cosmic Consciousness will deliver your expectations. Since it is an unlimited source of potential, it is best to release any ideas of limitations to your expected goal and be open to the infinity of possibilities.

Fear And Fearlessness

Because of the importance of fearlessness to successful detachment, I would like to explore it in a little more depth. Allow me to share a relevant story.

I have a friend, Loredana Popasav, who is an executive coach, and grew up in Romania under communism.[104] She told me that some time ago while visiting her mother's home in Transylvania, she discovered a photo of herself at age 10, on stage in the town square, dressed in a military uniform, surrounded by high-level military and political dignitaries. She was presenting to more than 2,000 people a 20-minute speech she had written for that occasion. She recalled it was an awesome and magical experience.

Everyone kept asking her if she was nervous, and she didn't understand why she should be. Loredana said, "I wasn't brave. It wasn't courage that got me going, but something better—the lack of fear." Just like a small infant, she didn't know enough to be afraid. That comes later in life, usually inadvertently and unintentionally from indoctrination by others who usually care deeply about you—parents, friends and teachers. She shared her opinion:

"Fearlessness is completely unremarkable. Courage is what most people think of when they hear the word fearlessness. Courage or bravery is when you're scared, but you'll do it anyway. Fearlessness, on the other hand, is the absence of fear, our natural state (think of that newborn). Throughout our lives we have learned to be fearful of certain things and the best thing we can think of against fear is courage. But, as super coach Michael Neill says, courage is nothing but a patch on fear. Courage says, 'Feel the fear and do it anyway.' Fearlessness says, 'What could happen, it's just a speech, it's just a marathon, it's just a pitch . . . It's not a big deal.'"

Loredana continued:

"It is fearlessness that takes us in the process of everything we want to accomplish, from desire to possibility to action. I therefore encourage you to look at whatever is in front of you from the perspective of fearlessness, from the understanding that the source of wellbeing, the very source of happiness is innate; it's inside you and it's not dependent on getting something, achieving something, or becoming something. Happiness is our natural state, is who we are, and is what we are made of."

The message here is to embrace your natural state of happiness, trust in the universe and have no fear—just let go, let it happen. It can and it will if you earnestly detach and enter a state of fearlessness.

In a way, you can look at a beautiful life—from birth to death—as the *Arc of Fearlessness*. You come into this world as a fearless child. If someone placed you in danger, for instance, next to a cliff, you would have no fear of falling over the side to your death. In time, society and human culture teaches you caution and fear, sometimes of value, such as, "Don't step off the cliff, you will die!"

But more often than that, the message can be paralyzing—"Do your job right, or you'll be fired!" However, if you unlearn useless fear and become an increasingly "awakened" person, then on that final day of this lifetime, you will likely think, "I love my life; I love what I have learned and what I have done; it has brought me great fulfillment; I am ready for the next step," and you will leave your body as a fearless adult; from birth to death in the *Arc of Fearlessness*.

The universe is an elegantly orchestrated symphony and it plays naturally and easily to one song, one verse; hence as stated earlier, we live in the "uni-verse." When our body, mind and spirit (Personal Consciousness) are in concert with the universe, everything comes to us spontaneously and effortlessly, and the energy of Cosmic Consciousness flows through us with the greatest of ease.

Road Blocks

There are only two factors that can get in the way of allowing the universe to do its thing in manifestations. The first is a social hypnosis based on deeply learned ideas from others as to how the world really *is* and how your life *can* be. The second challenging factor is ego gratification, namely responding to our indoctrination by society that success is based only on financial achievement and power status. This mode of pursuit, as discussed earlier, does not include what would be a third and most critical factor—service or Life Purpose to make the world a better place.

Absent these challenges, we discover that all we seek through manifestation can occur with the least effort, and everything in the universe is as it should be—in perfect harmony. Deepak Chopra calls this the Law of Least Effort.[105] It is reminiscent of the Principle of Least Action in classical physics, which governs all physical processes such as the path of a planet, the path of a stream of water or the path of a pulse of light. This law dictates that the path must always follow one of minimum time and energy to achieve a change.

Spiritual Physics shows us that this principle also applies to consciousness and to our efforts in manifestation.

When your world does not seem to be going the way you wish, whether you know it or not, it's always because you have chosen that path. Your free will is driven primarily by one of the factors discussed above. Your outcome is as it should be—to remain in concert with the laws of the universe and Spiritual Physics.

When you follow your Life Purpose path in all that you do, you are dancing to the rhythm of the cosmos and your life will unfold in comfort and ease. You no longer dwell on the socially-induced concept that fulfillment is the result of a constant struggle, namely, "no pain, no gain."

All of this distills down to a simple interpretation. We come into this world in the pure state of Personal Consciousness. But, we are like an onion; as we grow and progress in this hectic complex world, so does the diameter of the onion. We add additional shells of filters that cover our Personal Consciousness, which sits at our core. We must peel back these shells, as we would an onion in order to access our pure Personal Consciousness—a necessity to achieve detachment. Meditation is a wonderful tool to help accomplish this.

A final word of caution; do not discuss your intended manifestations with anyone until they are a proven fact. The primary reason is that others may be skeptical and only reinforce or rekindle your fear of failure. As you become increasingly successful in your manifestations, this cautionary point may be less important since you will have increased your self-confidence to achieve success. However, in general, I don't think this is a good idea.

Finally, it is important to express your gratitude for all that you currently have, first before your manifestation, and most certainly after success. This gratitude usually comes as a natural consequence of success, and it is a means of expressing not only thanks to the Cosmos, but also your continued commitment to the evolution of Cosmic Consciousness.

Yes You Can

As stated so well by Deepak Chopra's First Law of the Seven Spiritual Laws of Success—The Law of Pure Potentiality—"You can create anything, anytime, anywhere."[106]

This process works for manifestations where you have complete control of the necessary actions for example, losing weight. But it also works well for those where most of us might say we have little or no control for example, getting a job or a new home by the sea or meeting your soulmate.

The interface of *Intention, Attention, Imagination, Belief,* and *Detachment* intensifies the connection of Personal, Collective and Cosmic Consciousness. This enables all of the necessary forces of the universe to assemble and cooperate to achieve your goal.

These five steps may seem a bit contrived and cumbersome; however, I can promise you with no hesitation that with practice the process gets increasingly easier and the results come more quickly. What have you got to lose other than some time? The upside more than justifies the risk. Try it.

*"In silence you are
One within and without;
As above, so below."*

Chapter Ten

Finding Lifelong Fulfillment

"Life is not measured by the number of breaths we take, but by the moments that take our breath away."[107]

Vikki Corona, professional dancer

There may be other means to create lifelong fulfillment; however, I only know of one, and I know it works. This approach requires that you discover, understand and embrace your innate Essence and connect it to a Need in the world that makes it a better place in which to live. You will have then discovered your Life Purpose.

Your Essence is an intimate part of your Personal Consciousness (your soul, your Atman) and will never change, even as you progress through many reincarnations. But how you express your Life Purpose over time may well change. You may have leadership skills and start your professional career as an effective team player in a corporate setting, then advance to team leader, and because of your "Essential" talents, you may ultimately become a senior executive. In this sequence, your Life Purpose will change, but those special capabilities you were born with, namely your Essence, will never change. You may well refine and enhance them, but they will not change in any fundamental way. They are your inner core strengths, and they are with you for life.

Lifelong fulfillment requires that you follow your Life Purpose in a state of personal and professional Balance. Easily said, but how do you it?

Essence

It starts with your Essence. Everyone born into this world has one. Do you know what yours is, the one or two fundamental things you are really good at and love to do? If not, did you ever have even an inkling of what it is? It would likely have spoken to you when you were very young and not judgmental or swayed by the ways of the world, especially the prevailing archaic definition of success based on wealth and status.

I like to think of two broad categories of Essence, *hard* and *soft*. The former are strong technical capabilities in areas such as music, the arts, sports, math, science, mechanics, writing or computers. Soft or spiritual skills are as important as the hard ones, and in some cases, more important. They include attributes such as compassion, empathy, tenacity and emotional intelligence. Mother Theresa, Mahatma Gandhi, Bishop Tutu, Martin Luther King and Nelson Mandela are excellent examples of leaders who excelled in soft attributes. They changed the world for the better.

I am absolutely confident that you knew what your Essence was when you came into this world. I love the comment of Jalal ad-Din Muhammad Rumi, the 13th century Persian poet, theologian and Sufi mystic, *"Each of us is here for a particular work. The passion and desire for our intended work exist in our hearts from birth."* Recall from Chapter 4 my explanation of how I discovered my lifelong passion for science, technology and business at eight years of age and my predilection and capabilities in the field of entertainment when I was twelve. Of course, I didn't think in these terms at the time, but in retrospect, they were watershed events for me.

This same thing happens to each and every one of us. However, sometimes disclosure by the universe or more precisely, by Cosmic Consciousness, may be quite subtle; or it might entail a path that the more obvious aspects of our archaic definition of success do not support.

For example, you have always loved art and you're a natural born artist. As a youngster, you could draw and paint more creatively and captivatingly than anyone around you. Everyone could see and admire your talent. In high school you expressed a serious interest to study art and pursue it as your Life Purpose. However, the most common reprisal may well have been, "But, how will you make a *decent* living?"

If your personal character was easily swayed by those helping you to make the choice of your lifelong path—parents, teachers, friends—you may have missed all of the early signs and symbols of your Essence because of well-intended counsel and their guidance to a more "respectable and promising" pursuit. Even if you had chosen a so-called challenging profession, it may have been difficult for parents and friends to restrain themselves from offering what they truly believed were valuable critiques and assessments of your choice.

I would like to share a personal story. As a young girl, starting at about age five, my daughter Polly was deeply preoccupied with becoming an actress. We lived in Palo Alto, California, where movies were often filmed, and she would stand for hours on the sidelines observing the machinations of the filmmakers. If you have ever observed the tedium of making a movie, it can be quite boring to the uninitiated spectator. It's a bit like watching paint dry. But, for Polly, it was always an exciting adventure and inspiration to observe.

When she was finishing her sophomore year in high school, she announced that she wanted to become an actress and after graduation she would like to move to Los Angeles to launch her career. Although she appeared to have acting talent, to be completely frank, I was taken aback, but at the counsel of my wife I decided not to say a word against her intended pursuit. We both decided to support Polly emotionally in her chosen endeavor. I told her that if this was her true passion, she should go for it; however, I had only two important points to make. I sincerely and strongly advised her to go to college first, and second, she would have to support herself financially in her acting career.

She finally acquiesced and attended and graduated from Vassar College with a degree in filmmaking, as did Meryl Streep and several other famous Vassar-educated thespian alumni. After graduating from this prestigious college, she moved to Los Angeles where her first job, by choice, was as a waitress, so that she had the freedom and flexibility to take off from work for auditions.

Her career was challenging and sometimes painful. The statistics for the large majority of actors in the lower echelons are about a 5 percent success rate in getting roles for which they audition, and a 95 percent rejection rate with no feedback as to why they were not accepted. Rejection is a difficult demon for anyone to manage. That's the way of "Hollywood" for the vast majority of the actors and actresses living there.

But Polly persevered. She is clearly a talented actress, as she was admitted at age 23 after stringent audition requirements to the prestigious Los Angeles Actors Studio, where she mingled and honed her acting talents with the likes of Ellen Burstyn, Harvey Keitel, Al Pacino and Martin Landau. She worked in a number of movies as well as on stage and television shows, but never quite made it as they say in the business.

She is now happily married to a successful writer-director, and they have two lovely children. Polly has since "retired" from acting and is pursuing a new career based on another of her Essence talents in the arts—writing novels and screenplays.

As I looked back, I wondered if I should have violated my own philosophy and have told Polly to forget about acting, as it's almost always a troublesome proposition. I recently asked her if she felt she was successful. She said yes in that she learned a lot about people and the entertainment world that is helpful in her newly chosen path. She also is proud of her contributions to the film industry.

I asked her if she had it to do all over again, would she pursue a career in acting. Her response was "yes and no." Yes, because of what she learned and because it led to a happy marriage and two lovely children. No, because she feels that there are too many factors and people in charge of the creative process in filmmaking. She would want more control over the final product as the artist so that she could shape it to her vision.

This was an intense learning process for Polly, and had my wife and I dissuaded her from acting, she may still be wondering if acting should have been her outlet for the creative process she values so highly. Sometimes the process is a bit longer and arduous than you might have hoped for, but the final result can be overwhelmingly satisfying. Furthermore, it is likely that Polly's experience in acting will have an positive benefits in her new Life Purpose.

Polly's journey was not only a learning experience for her, but also for me; so much so, that when Julia, my youngest daughter was six months before birth, I wrote her a letter that was the result of my personal experience with Polly's acting career. My hope is that Julia will read it someday and learn something from her sister's and my experience. The letter is presented in appendix C.

If you know what your Essence is, that's great! If not, not to worry, you can find it and I will show you how to do that in the next section and how to link it to a need in the world and discover your Life Purpose.

Life Purpose

I see a serious global issue. Many people fail to recognize their Life Purpose. And in doing so, they fail to follow through on a journey of fulfillment and happiness. You can readily recognize the symptoms—aimlessness, depression, disengagement, poor performance and personal and professional economic turmoil. It absolutely need not be that way.

I love the quote by Mark Twain, which can be recast into an enlightening question. "What are the two most important days in your life?" Most everyone knows the answer to the first one—the day you were born—but not many guess the second—the day you find out why. That's when you finally connect your Essence with a Need in the world that gives something back and makes it a better place in which to live. You have found your Life Purpose. As Eckhart Tolle has noted in many of his lectures, *The fundamental question to ask yourself is not, "What do I want from life?" but more importantly, "What does life want from me?"*

Have you finally found and followed your Life Purpose, and if not, do you still know what it is? Did you follow the path intended for you by Cosmic Consciousness, or were you persuaded to do otherwise? If so, not to worry, you can always regain sound footing on your path; it is never too late to recover, understand and embrace what is intended for your destiny.

After a number of disconcerting missteps, Henry Ford started Ford Motor Company at age 40. Ray Croc launched McDonalds at 52 after numerous jobs ranging from café piano player to a traveling milkshake machine salesman. Colonel Harland Sanders meandered through his long life as an insurance salesman, a farmer, a steamboat operator and a filling station attendant before he decided to follow his lifelong passion for cooking, in particular, to commercialize his unique recipe for fried chicken. His initial recipe ultimately led to 18,000 stores in 120 countries.

Some are fortunate to break through at a somewhat younger age, albeit not without significant challenges. J. K. Rowling was 32, working as a secretary, barely making a living following several serious personal setbacks, when she completed her first Harry Potter novel. Interestingly, her manuscript was rejected by the first 12 publishers she approached. She persisted and found her Life Purpose. Rowling is currently the 12th wealthiest woman in the United Kingdom and a generous philanthropist.[108] She never set out to become wealthy; the Harry Potter novels were an expression of her driving deep passion for writing.

It's all about Life Purpose. Properly pursued, it always leads to fulfillment, and more often than not to financial rewards, even though that is almost never the focus of someone on their Life Purpose path.

What is lifelong fulfillment? It certainly is not eternal bliss. Essentially no one is blessed with a state of constant happiness. Your dog dies; you have a fender-bender auto accident; you damage your knee skiing; someone close to you dies. These things happen, even to the best of people. For me, fulfillment is a feeling of contentment, joy and personal satisfaction, and is not experienced 24 hours per day, unless perhaps you are a wise guru living alone in a deep meditative state in a cave in the Himalayas. The great majority of us are not like that.

However, when you look back over a week, a month, a year, and certainly at that last moment, hopefully well into the future when your spirit is about to leave your body, you want to be able to say with complete honesty and sincere satisfaction, "I have lived well; I love my life; I love what I've done. I am deeply grateful." How can we be sure that this will be the final outcome?

Over the years, I have assembled eight questions that if truthfully answered, will inevitably uncover your Essence and Life Purpose. These questions are easy to ask, but challenging to answer with deep unfettered personal truth. The correct answers are those inside you, and not outside—not responses that someone advises or influences you as to what the answers should be. Also, the answer to any one question may not uncover you Life Purpose, but the composite answers to all eight questions will provide a provocative and inspiring perspective that most certainly will.

The very best way to discover the answers is to ask the questions just prior to entering a deeply relaxed and preferably meditative state. You already know the answers inside at your very core, within your Personal Consciousness. It's just a matter of peeling back the filters to see and hear them. Meditation does this. It allows you to connect directly and intimately with your Personal Consciousness and with Cosmic Consciousness, and thereby find your personal truth. The answers should not be what you superficially want them to be, or think they should be. They should come from your soul and constitute your real truth.

I would advise you not to expect answers immediately; just ask the questions and be patient; you will move into the answers. It may take a day, a week, or a month; but you will definitely get the answers to your questions. If you are deeply committed to the process, I guarantee that it will not let you down. You will experience a deep sense of relief, satisfaction and a passion for the future.

Once you have the answers to most, if not all of the questions, you will have a map of your destiny. You will look at that template and think about the implications of the answers. With pen and paper in hand you will brainstorm on the abundance of possibilities based on your map. One of those possibilities will speak to you and it will incite a deep passion as you have probably never experienced before.

This kind of passion opens up clear channels of communication between the left and right hemispheres of your brain, providing an incredible synergy between the complements of intense creativity and accurate analysis. Your new-found creativity will enable you to innovatively address issues that would have previously seemed insurmountable. You are well on your way to pursuing your Life Purpose and the ultimate gratitude and fulfillment that this journey delivers.

Eight Questions

Here are the eight questions and examples of how they may play out in certain specific circumstances.[109]

1. **What interest do you fear to pursue?** You recall with fondness that as a teenager you had a significant talent to design and produce high-fashion clothes for yourself, family and friends. They loved your creations and you loved creating them. You currently work in a bank and the job is fine, but unexciting for you personally. You hardly have time anymore to do the fine tailoring you did years ago. You have occasional thoughts of opening up your own shop to design and make custom clothes. But your immediate response is almost always, "Oh, what a crazy idea! How would I ever get started? I might fail and then what would I do?" You have a whole list of reasons why you should not pursue what might be your life dream and Life Purpose.

2. **What do you love about yourself?** Don't be concerned about your ego. You're speaking strictly to you, and for a very good intention and reason. At work, when there is turmoil among your colleagues, you have an excellent knack for listening carefully to understand all sides and helping them reach an equitable and fair compromise. Everyone walks away content and grateful for your intervention. You love that you are able to make this contribution; it's a prized element of

emotional intelligence and a strong leadership skill, and is most valuable in any number of circumstances. This is the kind of skill that has significant leverage in helping people to be as great as they really can and should be. You are a born leader.

3. **What do you love to do such that time passes so quickly?** You love to tinker with all kinds of machines and devices. Since you were a youngster, you have had an uncanny intuitive mechanical capability that enables you to fix just about anything. When working on your car or on installing a new sound system throughout your apartment or home, you easily forget lunch or dinner. Such innate mechanical skills may have application in a large number of technical professions.

4. **What work do you not consider work?** When I was in my freshman year of high school, through a series of coincidences—I don't believe in coincidences—I was offered a part-time job after school as a laboratory technician helping a successful inventor in his development of chemically-based products for home and industry. It was so much fun because of my interest in chemistry, and I was learning so much, I would have worked there for free. Science and technology have thrilled me for as long as I can remember.

5. **Who does something you can do and would love to do?** I know a young woman who is a lawyer, lives in New York City and works for a large multinational corporation. Some years ago, she rediscovered her passion for something she was good at since her childhood—comedy. She performs occasionally throughout the month, when not traveling, as a standup comedienne at well-know improvisation night clubs in Manhattan. The comedians work for free there with the hope of being discovered for the "big time." She could easily see herself as the host of one of those late-night variety shows. She is now working with an executive coach to help her decide on how to make a huge professional life change.

6. **What could you do to create the greatest value for the world around you and the greatest personal satisfaction?** Allow me to share a personal experience in our family that could have worked out this way, but unfortunately did not.

   Growing up as the oldest of 10 children, my father, who was a postman, had to work part-time jobs at night and on weekends to supplement his income, and even at that, life was an economic struggle for our family.

   A promising potential venture occurred quite naturally when my mom, who is an incredible Italian cook, started making pizzas in a set of old ovens in my grandparents' basement and selling them in our neighborhood. My mom and sisters baked the pizzas and my brothers and I helped my father deliver them.

   We charged 50 percent more than what customers would pay to have what we called an "Americana" pizza delivered by the neighborhood pizzeria. Our pizzas were an authentic Italian recipe, tasty and made with lots of love from the healthiest natural ingredients. Our customers also loved kibitzing with my dad, who was a charismatic entertaining delivery man.

   A few months into our family venture, the neighborhood pizza restaurant went up for sale and a friend of my father's offered to buy it and make him a partner if he and my mom would run it. In Dad's friend's mind, there was no way it could fail and in fact would likely do really well. He had the financial resources and experience necessary to keep the business on track. We also had access to lots of inexpensive kitchen help and waiters from brothers and sisters and me!

   To the deep disappointment of my mom, brothers, sisters and me, my father turned down the opportunity, even though he disliked his job at the post office. To his way of thinking, the post office was a sure thing until retirement and essentially no financial risk. He unfortunately regretted his decision for many years afterwards. With his charismatic marketing personality—his Essence—and my mother's creative Italian cooking—her Essence—I, like most of our family and friends, believed it would have been a rousing success. The project would not only have been financially beneficial, but equally important, it would have made a significant contribution to the neighborhood and my dad and my mom would have found their Passion and Life Purpose. But, unfortunately, it wasn't to be.

We lost the opportunity because of my father's challenge with an issue that all of us face at one time or another—the fear of failure.

7. **Which of your skills could provide benefits to your organization, to the world and to you?** Sometimes it may not be your primary skill, but still of important value. I offer a personal story concerning my early experience as an entertainer and its "corporate" value during the fledgling beginnings of Catalytica, the high-tech company I cofounded.[110]

When my partners and I were raising venture capital for the first time, we sought a valuation 20 percent higher than the investing venture group was willing to pay. The day before we were to finalize negotiations, I met with the managing director of a second venture firm that was interested in putting money into our company. Over dinner, my business partner mentioned my prior career in music. The gentleman suddenly exclaimed, "Now I know why you look so familiar; I saw you some years ago on Dick Clark's American Bandstand TV Show in Philadelphia. That's just fantastic! Would you be willing to sing for our annual venture party?" The next day his company contributed 50 percent of our funding and both venture groups agreed to our 20 percent higher valuation.

8. **What's stopping your decision?** What are you afraid of? What's really the worst thing that could happen? My experience over many years is that anyone who consistently uses

his or her Essence to follow their Life Purpose always has a job, even in cases where for whatever reason a particular exploit doesn't work out. Working in Silicon Valley for more than 25 years, I saw this happen more times than I could count. Don't let fear strangle your discovery of your Essence, your Life Purpose and your Passion.

So, once you know your Essence and Life Purpose; go for it! Start thinking how things will work out, and not why they won't. Use the *Law of Manifestation* and the power of the **Attention—Intention—Imagination—Belief—Detachment** coupling to create the life you dream of, the life you deserve, the life the universe was destined to give you.

The Children Challenge

Before we move on, I think it useful to briefly address a key challenge most often faced by mothers, but also sometimes by stay-at-home fathers.

You graduated from college; you were recruited by a prestigious multinational firm; you moved up the ranks with rapid promotions, met and fell in love with a gentleman colleague, a senior executive at the firm; you married and had your first child, a lovely little girl named Gena.

You took maternity leave for several months, but now you're torn between playing a major role in raising Gena and any other children you and your husband may have; or hiring an *au pair* to take over a large part of your role at home, while you return to work. There is no easy right or wrong answer to this conundrum, and the one you must follow is the one that rests in your soul and is based on personal values that are important to you.

However, there is a key insight that many mothers often do not appreciate. Yes, they know that their presence and guidance is important to their children, and those qualities cannot be fully replaced by an *au pair*. They may also have a deep-seated feeling and passion that they must follow their professional path to share their creative contributions for a better world. This is why many mothers struggle much of their professional life trying to live essentially two full-time passions.

I wish to raise two points. First, you likely have, as many mothers do, several of the key soft Essences, namely compassion, empathy, listening and service orientation; and you have all of the skills necessary to make a huge contribution to the world by raising a successful and productive child into adulthood. When considered in its deepest sense, few accomplishments cast a shadow over such an achievement. Children are our real future. They will inherit our world and hopefully do their best to make it better.

There is also an emerging scientific perspective that many of us neither recognize, nor do we understand its power and potential. It is based on the science of epigenetics. In brief, it has now been proven by numerous research studies that the environment you create for your child can and will impact his or her genes—permanently—for better or for worse. In other words, the human genome is not fixed at birth. It develops further even after birth, especially during the first decade, but even after that period as well. Your children's genes are not static and fixed.

This means what you do, what you say, and the environment that you expose your child to during the course of their maturation from infancy into their teens will profoundly shape their skills, capabilities and likely, their success as an adult. I raise these points to underscore the critical importance that parenthood (both motherhood and fatherhood) has, not just on your child's personality, but right down to the genetics that make them who they really are and who they will be in the future.

What could be a more important, challenging and creative job? Our socially-controlled culture does not allow mothers or fathers to truly, deeply and accurately understand and appreciate the value of such a contribution. Socially recognized successes are generally professional successes, not necessarily parental ones.

My intent here is not to make a biased case for motherhood exclusive of a professional career. Instead, I want to recognize the significant value that those mothers who have the talent to flourish in a professional career, yet choose to focus completely on raising their children.

I have a personal story to exemplify an outcome related to this challenge. My oldest daughter, Doreen, was an excellent student throughout her school years. She received her degree in business administration and then immediately passed the Certified Public Accountant exam in California and was recruited by PricewaterhouseCoopers as a tax accountant.

Doreen quickly became one of their "in-demand" tax accountants within Silicon Valley, where there are numerous wealthy entrepreneurs seeking to creatively and legally protect their income from the U.S. Internal Revenue Service.

When her first child was born, she made a well-thought-out decision that she and her husband would likely have a couple more children and she would commit her full-time efforts to support them emotionally and academically from infancy through completion of their college degrees. It was her choice, based on her personal values, and certainly was not made flippantly. Doreen's husband assured her that he was supportive of her decision, regardless of which way she chose to proceed.

A quick assessment of her children's progress provides an interesting retrospective. All three children are natively intelligent, but we all know that is not enough for a path to success and fulfillment.

Doreen's personal commitment to day-to-day and year-to-year academic and after-school activities support, I believe, significantly contributed to their successes. The oldest daughter became an accomplished figure skater, but after severely damaging her ankle, transitioned to become one of the top amateur women golfers in the U.S.; she graduated from Harvard—Harvard recruited her because of her academic and golf skills.—and now she will attend medical school. The middle daughter, a talented soccer player is a third-year student at the prestigious Cornell School for Hotel Administration. And the youngest child, a boy, has also demonstrated academic and sports excellence and is a member of one of the top beach volley-ball teams in California.

I raise these examples because I witnessed firsthand over the years how Doreen's commitment, based obviously on deep moth-erly love and commitment, but also strengthened by compassion, attentiveness and selfless service, played an important role in the past, current and very likely future success of all three children.

I have seen many mothers help create similar paths of success for their children. While not wanting to detract from the children's native intelligence and their personal drive to succeed, my point is that motherly love and support during formative years is a much more pro-found personal and social accomplishment than we often give credit to. It changes our challenged world for the better and provides greater hope for a sustainable future. It would be beneficial if our culture were to give much greater recognition to these contributions.

Balance

Discovering, understanding and embracing your *Essence*, then con-necting it with a *Need* in the world to make it a better place will implement your *Life Purpose* and ignite all of the *Passion, Energy*, Creativity and Innovation you require to lead to a successful path to *Gratitude* and intense *Fulfillment*, but not to lifelong fulfillment. That requires one additional key factor—*Balance*—A balance between your professional and your personal endeavors.

As nearly everyone knows, in this fast-moving, interconnected and often chaotic world, Balance is one of the most difficult things to achieve. But it need not be. There is a way to have both simul-taneously, Balance and Life Purpose, and therefore, Lifelong Fulfillment. First, we must agree on the definition of Balance.

For me, *Balance is the application of optimal effort towards admirable and worthwhile goals that you set for yourself in both your personal and pro-fessional spheres.* Optimal means that your strategy and its implemen-tation in both your personal and professional lives are such that you exercise enough effort to achieve your goals in both areas in a timely manner. The goals are your goals; they may be challenging, but you have 100 percent ownership of them. And if they are challenging, they are also achievable in your mind. So the overarching objective is to have rewards in both arenas.

I know of no effective way to accomplish this without the intimate meshing of two things: a values-based life plan and effective time and energy management of the process. Anything else is wishful thinking and running through life with minimal guidance, alternate experiences of excitement and fear, and ultimately often falling short of your intended outcomes.

There is one other possible means to accomplish Lifelong Fulfillment. However, it is a deeply spiritual path and usually those who elect to proceed on this journey inevitably give up friends, family and most of their material possessions and focus only on enlightenment. This way is not for everyone; in fact, it is really only for those who are already well down the road to enlightenment.

How do you know if you're out of balance and to what degree? I offer you 10 questions, the answers to which will stimulate your thinking as to just how much you are either in or out of balance.

1. How are your physical and emotional energies?
2. Do you see the value you bring to the world?
3. Do you put sufficient effort into those areas you truly value?
4. Do you manage your health?
5. Are you growing personally and professionally?
6. Do you understand and support your company's strategy?
7. Do you provide input on issues concerning your job?
8. Are you aware of the impact of your efforts on your firm's progress?
9. Do you feel trusted by managers, colleagues, family and friends?
10. Have you taken time to follow your dream?

If you answer each of these questions honestly, not how you hope to be, you will have a good qualitative estimate of your sense of personal-professional balance.

Values-Based Life Plan[111]

To create a values-based life plan means that you must first determine those values by which you wish to live your life. They are your true values, and come from deep within your soul and are not what you or anyone else may think your values are. That's wishful thinking and not reality. In a moment of truth—I suggest that you use the tools of relaxation and meditation to help you in this process. There is no right or wrong in this process, just what really *is* important to how you live your life!

There are six value areas that are important to most people who want to create Lifelong Fulfillment. I am assuming that you are clear on your *soft* criteria such as compassion, integrity and empathy, and they are integrated across all six value area. The six Fundamental Value Areas are as follows:

1. **Professional**—You have discovered your *Essence* and a need in the world that would benefit from your capabilities. In the profession that you pursue, how do you want to work? What is important to you in the way that you do your job? Areas to consider are travel, location, social networking, culture, people, goals, multitasking, continuous learning and company size.

2. **Financial**—How important is money to you? How much do you need to live the life you dream? Do you intend to give some away?

3. **Relationships**—Who are the most important people in your life and how do you want to spend time with them?

4. **Spiritual**—What spiritual endeavors are important to you— religion, yoga, social and cultural causes, meditation, charity, journey to enlightenment, etc.?

5. **Health**—How will you take care of your physical body— food, drink, sleep, exercise?

6. **Knowledge**—Life is a continuous learning journey. What do you want to study and learn?

For each of these value areas, write down one long-term goal. A few examples might be something like this, "For my Professional long-term goal, I will start a successful company in architectural design. For my Health long-term goal, I will weigh 70 kilograms (154 pounds), run a half-marathon, and have positive results for my annual medical exam. For my Financial long-term goal, I will have no debt and $1 million in the bank or investments so that I can live self-sufficiently for the rest of my life according to the personal lifestyle I have chosen." Long-term goals can be set for all six areas.

Next, for each of these six areas you can write down approximately three goals for each of the next three years. Then, for the current year only, write down a set of actions you will take, and where at all possible, the date during the year at which the specific actions will be completed.

In addition to balancing your time, you must balance your energy use. For example, if you have certain professional goals that require peak energy such as direct sales, they should not be implemented at the expense of personal goals that also require energy, such as one hour of quality time with your children in the evening after dinner. If you provide peak energy to prospective clients or customers, you must also find the means to physically and emotionally recover so that you have ample physical and emotional energy left for play with your children if that is one of your values. You must manage both, time and energy—not an easy task, but immensely rewarding.[112]

You now have a long-term life plan which is driven by a rolling three-year plan with specific emphasis on goals and actions within the current year. This plan is then updated at the beginning of every New Year. It takes quite some work to do this the first time, but subsequent years are much easier as they generally require only refinements, and the subsequent goals and actions become increasingly obvious to you.

It is very important to be brutally open and honest with yourself as to what's truly important to you and what your want to achieve. The meditation process is a valuable tool for helping you to "peel back each layer of the onion" to see, feel, hear, taste and touch your true self which is at your very core. An alternate form of meditation, which I call *kinetic meditation*, can also be helpful in this process. It involves long solitary walks in the quiet of nature, through the forest or along the sea, or perhaps, a long candle-lit warm bath.

Your final plan may require a number of pages. You should clearly study it periodically to be sure that you are on track. I have found it helpful to distill in some form of shorthand, the key goals and actions for the current year and place them on my smart phone. Look at the plan at least once a week. You will be amazed at the progress you will make and will revel in your accomplishments. It's the power of the pen when connected to the omniscience and omnipotence of the soul, Personal Consciousness.

You cannot successfully command enthusiasm, purpose, passion, creativity and innovation. These are gifts that people find within themselves; they emerge from their very soul—Personal Consciousness; and they use these gifts if and only if they are fully engaged and passionate in their pursuit of fulfillment. When they succeed in their journey, they find that fulfillment is found when they have negotiated the path I have described earlier. Following your Life Purpose with Balance is what leads to lifelong fulfillment.

As you journey through life, whether at home, work or play, why not seek to be an inspirational person and create an environment that helps you and others find and follow their Life Purpose with Balance? Many will gladly follow and support you, as you change the world for the better. You will experience the deepest sense of personal gratitude. That's really what long-term fulfillment is all about.

*"You are meant to be
Fulfilled. Just Be,
And it will be so."*

EPILOGUE

"You may say I'm a dreamer, but I'm not the only one. I hope someday you'll join us. And the world will live as one."[113]

John Lennon (1940-1980), singer-songwriter

T he 12 Universal Rules have broad implications for the way both you and the universe function. Understanding these Rules and diligently applying them and the results and implications that follow from them will enable you to use your understanding of the *Meaning of Life* to create the life you have always dreamed of, both here and hereafter.

You are part of a greater purpose, not only for your continuous physical and consciousness evolution, but also for the continuous evolution of Cosmic Consciousness, namely God, of which you are an intimate part. *Yes, God is within you.* That is an incredible gift and equally, an incredible responsibility. And with attentive responsibility comes the benefits of this gift, well beyond your greatest expectations.

In a journey backwards in time, you can rediscover what Eastern philosophy has been earnestly teaching us for millennia—Cosmic Consciousness is the unlimited consciousness that permeates creation and resides as the core existence, intelligence and love within each of us in the form of our Personal Consciousness. In this respect, God truly is an all-pervasive super-intelligence that unites everything in the universe. Every person, in fact, everything, has always been and always will be intimately connected. Cosmic Consciousness is responsible for the infinite eternal connectivity, unity and *Universal Wholeness.*

Depending on the level of consciousness, the intensity of this interconnectedness may vary among people, species and inanimate things. However, connectivity grows in intensity as Cosmic Consciousness progresses with its evolution. This is part of our exquisite, elegant and eternal cosmic dance together, our journey together toward greater and greater *Oneness.*

To understand the essence underpinning the insights discussed here—to digest that essence, to challenge it, and then to discover your personal truth as a distillation of this process—can only be accomplished though a personal internal journey of inquiry. That journey is best carried out through a consistent and dedicated practice of meditation, whatever form you choose—prayer, deep solitude, walks in nature, or any other form of an elevated state of "normal" consciousness.

As you travel this journey, ask yourself simple, yet profound questions. *Who am I? What is my purpose? What do I truly want? What is the contribution I want to make to this world? What are my special talents? How can I use these talents to serve humanity and the universe?*

In asking these questions, don't look for immediate answers. Live with the questions and in due time, with seemingly no effort, you will move into the answers. This I promise, as long as you pursue them with full integrity on a consistent path. As the answers arise within you, they will profoundly change your life.

Pondering them, you may rightfully be perplexed, but at a certain moment, also amazed at the mysteries and paradoxes that grace the realm of your Personal Consciousness and the universal intelligence and spirit of Cosmic Consciousness.

Deepak Chopra tells us that "God is both transcendent and immanent at the same time. God could be considered outside us in the sense that God is transcendent to all aspects of our relative identity. But in another sense, God is our deepest essence and therefore is more intimate to us than our very thoughts."[114]

This is why we often say that human potential is well beyond our wildest dreams. You are truly special. All of us are. And when you bypass the distractions of your ego and touch your deepest core, your Personal Consciousness, you will realize that you can do anything and manifest anything within the realm of infinite possibilities offered to you through the laws of Spiritual Physics.

And so, we come to the most fundamental, most important insight and conclusion concerning all of humanity. God is within each of us and within all things, everywhere. This is the source of our unlimited power and possibilities.

To truly know God and access this gift, in quiet meditation we must look deep inside ourselves. We will then recognize, but more importantly, *know* and *feel* our Personal Consciousness through its connection to the Collective Consciousness of the universe, to all others, animate and inanimate. All are intimately embraced by God.

In following this path, you cannot help but internalize and understand the true *Meaning of Life* and thereby unleash your power, a power you possess at this very moment inside you, to create the *Life You Dream.*

Then, you will have truly discovered that *Life Is Beautiful.*

Appendix A
Prayer To St. Francis[115]

Lord,[5] make me an instrument of thy peace,
Where there is hatred, let me sow love;
Where there is injury, pardon;
Where there is discord, harmony;
Where there is error, truth;
Where there is doubt, faith;
Where there is despair, hope;
Where there is darkness, light;
Where there is sadness, joy.

O divine Master, grant that
I may not so much seek
To be consoled as to console,
To be understood as to understand,
To be loved as to love;
For it is in giving that we receive;
It is in pardoning that we are pardoned;
It is in dying that we are born to eternal life.

---

5 The words "Lord" and "Master" do not refer to a regal white-bearded man sitting on a throne somewhere in the heights of "heaven above," but rather to our Personal Consciousness, the True Divine Self that resides within each of us.

APPENDIX B
THE 12 UNIVERSAL RULES OF LIFE

RULE #1—EVERYTHING BEGINS AND ENDS WITH COSMIC CONSCIOUSNESS.

Cosmic Consciousness is a universal intelligent energy field that is infinite and eternal. It is omnipotent, omnipresent and omniscient. Its sole purpose is to evolve continuously and infinitely towards ever increasing collective knowledge, awareness, connectedness and Oneness. Our purpose is to facilitate and participate in the joy and pleasure of this infinite evolutionary process. This role requires both our physical and spiritual (consciousness) bodies.

⊗

RULE #2—THERE ARE THREE ELEMENTS OF CONSCIOUSNESS. THEY ARE SEPARATE, YET ONE.

The totality of consciousness throughout the universe consists of Personal Consciousness (yours, mine, and that of others); Collective Consciousness, that which is associated with the intimate interaction of all material entities in the universe; and Cosmic Consciousness. Paradoxically, all are separate and yet, intimately embraced by each other.

RULE #3—YOUR SUBCONSCIOUS CREATES YOUR OBSERVED REALITY.

The cooperative interaction of Cosmic, Collective and Personal Consciousness is the source of all intelligent activity in the universe. The intimacy, yet separateness of these three elements of consciousness initiates, orchestrates and terminates every physical and spiritual event that occurs in the universe. All is created subjectively by the subconscious with no judgment of morality, ethics or otherwise.

RULE #4—CONSCIOUSNESS IS YOUR TRUE REALITY.

Consciousness is your complete ground of being. It is your True Reality, not the mirage you perceive with your five senses. Your conscious observation brings the universe and everything in it into reality as experienced by your five senses. This is known as the Observer Effect, and without it the universe and all its contents would be a sea of an infinite number of energy vibrational waves, each characteristic of a unique possible universe and its contents. Your observation collapses this infinite number into one possibility, the one you observe with your five senses. This collapse to a single universe described by one wave equation is called Decoherence.

RULE #5—THE UNIVERSE AND OUR TRUE REALITY ARE NOT WHAT WE PERCEIVE WITH OUR FIVE SENSES.

The universe is an interdependently co-arising confluence of space-time events, omnipresent in infinite time—past, present, and future, in an infinite field of consciousness that is beyond space-time, meaning there is no beginning and no end. The universe encompasses all the events that have ever occurred, are occurring, and all that will ever occur. As incomprehensible as it may seem, all has co-arisen together. There is no such thing as time in the consciousness world, and the universe continues to arise and subside, ad infinitum into eternal Infinite Absolute Nothingness.

RULE #6—PERSONAL CONSCIOUSNESS CATALYZES AND MANAGES YOUR JOURNEY TO ENLIGHTENMENT.

Personal Consciousness is not only your true reality, but also your infinite existence, and as such it is your spirit. Though not physically tangible, it is spiritually tangible. Your physical presence is but a momentary station-stop on your journey to enlightenment, namely perfect eternal fulfillment. So, by any definition, your Personal Consciousness is your true self. It manages your journey to enlightenment by the Law of Karmic Action.

RULE #7—CONSCIOUSNESS PRESCRIBES YOUR PATH TO YOUR FULFILLMENT IN THE PHYSICAL WORLD.

Your ability to experience long-term joy and happiness in the five-sense physical world is intimately connected to and guided by your Personal Consciousness, and can be described by a simple, but profound path known as the Path to Fulfillment.

RULE #8—CONSCIOUSNESS IS INFINITE AND ETERNAL AND EVOLVES TO AN INCREASING LEVEL OF WHOLENESS THROUGH EXPANSION OF A SUBATOMIC SINGULARITY.

The infinite presence of consciousness has always existed and penetrates the universe, as well as the eternal Infinite Absolute Nothingness that surrounds the universe. Consciousness continues to evolve and progress ad infinitum through rapid expansion of what is called a subatomic singularity. It contains all of the matter and energy that has ever existed and that will ever exist.

RULE #9—THROUGH EXPANSION AND CONTRACTION CYCLES OF THE BIG BANG SINGULARITY, CONSCIOUSNESS EVOLVES TOWARDS INCREASINGLY GREATER LEVELS OF COLLECTIVE ONENESS.

The purpose of alternate expansions and contractions of the universe is a means to continuously evolve Cosmic Consciousness. This is God's progressive evolution towards greater Oneness with all.

RULE #10—EVERYTHING IN THE UNIVERSE IS CONNECTED AT THE LEVEL OF CONSCIOUSNESS.

Each subsequent singularity contains the same amount of mass and energy as the previous one, but it is further evolved in consciousness than the prior singularity. It also has a cosmic "imprint" that leads to the continued advance of physical and spiritual evolution with each new cycle. This process will continue forever. Because all of the mass and energy in the universe was in intimate contact within the singularity before its expansion, quantum entanglement tells us that everything in the universe is connected.

RULE #11—LOVE, THE STRONGEST FORCE IN THE UNIVERSE, ENABLES ALL CONSCIOUS ENTITIES TO INTERACT FOR THE BENEFIT OF THE WHOLE.

Love is the catalytic force that enables all things to interact for the benefit of the "Whole" as it navigates the evolutionary journey of Personal, Collective and Cosmic Consciousness towards Oneness. Perfect love is a deep combination of the following: collective awareness of, selfless concern and compassion for, cooperation with, and a commitment to all other entities in the universe. For pragmatic evolutionary reasons, not sensual or sexual ones, it is the most potent force in the universe.

RULE #12—ADDRESSING COMPLEX SOCIAL AND CULTURAL CHALLENGES REQUIRES AN APPROPRIATE DYNAMIC BALANCE BETWEEN MASCULINE AND FEMININE ENERGIES.

As social units progress and evolve, an increasing ratio of feminine to masculine energies is required. This evolution is a transition from a primary focus on protection from predators and provision for food and shelter, to intimate sensitivity to social and cultural complexities. This necessitates increased focus on human compassion, win-win negotiations, rapid intuitive assessment of complex systems and deep sensitivity to multidimensional social factors such as culture, gender, race and emotional intelligence. This is the domain of the Sacred Feminine, which is always committed to success of the Whole.

Appendix C
A Letter to Julia[116]

"Will you still need me, will you still feed me, when I'm sixty four?"[117]
John Lennon/Paul McCartney, The Beatles

Dearest Julia:

Although you're several months from struggling out of a comfortable cocoon in mom's belly, into this exciting and challenging world, I have a few thoughts I am eager to share with you. I guess the miracle of your coming into our lives is the beginning of a new and exciting adventure for me. I honestly feel like a kid again.

I hope that someday if you read this letter, you don't think of me as an overbearing and preachy father, as I express some of my experiences, views, and hopefully leave you with at least a spark of wisdom to think about. Perhaps there is something here that will be helpful to you as you travel your life's journey.

⚜ ⚜ ⚜

I would guess, Julia, that most of my friends would say I have led an eclectic—some might say hectic life. But I can honestly say that I deeply value the experiences that have crossed my life path over the years, and trust that I have learned from them, and hopefully left a few good marks along the way.

As a young boy, growing up during the 1950s on the streets of Elizabeth, New Jersey, I wore the typical teenage uniform of the day—Levis, strapped with a black, big-buckled, chrome-studded belt, a white tee shirt, motorcycle boots, a black leather jacket, and dark, aviator sunglasses carefully perched on my nose at just the right angle. My hair was slicked back with Brylcreeme®, decorated with a small spit-curl at the top of my forehead, *a la* "Bill Haley & The Comets" of "Rock Around The Clock" fame. That was *the* style of the 1950s "in-crowd."

My friends and I did lots of normal guy things. We played stick-ball, kick-the-can, and curb-ball in the street, and football, basket-ball and baseball at an empty lot near your great-grandmother's two-family home where we lived at the time. It was there I was born and lived for the first 15 years of my life. My friends and I went on "safaris," hunting snakes and rats with homemade bamboo spears and slingshots in the dense North Elizabeth meadowlands, an area that one day would give way to the runways for Newark International Airport.

On occasion, I confess, we resorted to dangerous pastimes, like jumping from one tenement roof to the next, hopping slow-moving freight trains at the nearby Pennsylvania Railroad yard, or walking narrow wooden planks, loosely strung between the windows of abandoned tenement buildings. It makes me shudder to even think about some of those crazy undertakings. By some miracle of destiny, I somehow survived those times.

If I had seen even a glimpse of my future, I would never have believed it. I hadn't the faintest idea—that is, consciously—that I would eventually become a recording artist; a physical chemist; a research executive for the world's largest oil company; cofounder and chairman of a billion-dollar, high-tech, public company; founder and CEO of a feature film production company; and more recently with mom, owner of Chateau Mcely, an award-winning, castle hotel and spa in the Czech Republic providing a holistic experience of body, mind and spirit to people from all over the world. Five forks in the road, five different lives—who would have guessed?

Julia, please don't think that your dad is a mental giant. I'm not. Nor, do I want you to think that this was all luck. It wasn't. Yes, I worked passionately, diligently and tenaciously all of my life. But, my life unfolded this way because it was my calling, my Life Purpose. Fortunately, by listening to a number of those special guides we all meet throughout our life, I heard the invitation.

Equally important, I recognized a few key opportunities at critical crossroads—some might call them omens. But in all honesty, at those junctures, as Sir Isaac Newton was fond of saying, "I stood on the shoulders of giants,"—a few incredibly talented people. They were people who really made *the* difference in my life—men and women, more intelligent, more experienced and certainly more evolved than I. They were there when I needed them, and they wholeheartedly embraced me and my ideas. A few special friends made a world of difference for me, and people like this will be there for you too. I am sure of it. But you must listen carefully to recognize these few people and the omens at the crossroads in your life, and what they portend for your future.

I'm not suggesting that you follow in my footsteps, or that you even entertain such a diverse multiplicity of roles in your life. I don't think that approach is necessarily the best for a successful and fulfilling life's journey. If it comes your way, fine. If not, that's fine, too. I have seen in the lives of others that a single focus can be equally fascinating and rewarding, quite often, more so.

But I strongly suggest that you listen for the omens and follow your life purpose, your passion and your heart tenaciously, whether your dream is to be a scientist, a banker, a doctor or a carpenter. And Julia, the key words here are *purpose, passion* and *tenacity*. In my opinion, they are always the driving forces behind any real success in this world. Always treasure the freedom you have in making your choices in life, and of course take personal responsibility for your decisions.

I'm not saying that success will come your way without a dedicated, diligent and focused effort. You must work hard to get *there*, and *there* will always move further into the future, as you set new goals and objectives to replace the ones you achieve. As far as I'm concerned, that is the best definition of success—following your Life Purpose to achieve admirable worthwhile goals that you continually set for yourself and that make this world a little better place in which to live.

If the engine for your journey is fueled by your purpose, passion and tenacity, you will not only get "there," but you will enjoy the ride. So yes, you must be a doer and work hard for your success. But that still leaves open the pertinent and provocative question, "What do I do?" Here, I offer you a way to think about this. It's simple to state, but so challenging to do.

At the conscious level, we really have no idea what the universe has in store for us. For many people this can be frightening, and yet for some, it's exhilarating. I suggest that you let your life unfold according to the possibilities that are already written on the pages of your destiny, and are well known within your subconscious.

You have come into this world for a specific purpose, something that when pursued will make it a better place in which to live, so don't be afraid. As you listen inside to your true self and discover your Life Purpose, set your goals, and then proceed to achieve them, letting your intuition lead the way. It is your personal compass, your *true north*, and it's connected to the soul of the universe.

What I'm saying, Julia, is always follow your inner voice—your deepest intuition. In moments of quiet contemplation, some might call it "meditation," it is your intuition that enhances and strengthens the bond of communion between your spirit and that of the universe. This is why all things are connected. For I can assure you, they are. Don't let anyone convince you otherwise.

This connectivity has been espoused for thousands of years in Eastern Wisdom, and based on findings of modern quantum physics, increasingly more scientists are coming to the same conclusion. But that's another long and complex story. I think until the majority of us come to grips with the fundamental truth of connectivity among all things—tangible and intangible—there can be no everlasting peace on this planet.

"There is no real distinction between your consciousness and somebody else's consciousness. And this is not mumbo jumbo philosophy; it emerges from our understanding of basic neuroscience."[118]

Allow me to show you how this omen thing works. For me, the first critical omen in my life appeared when I was almost nine years of age. It was a Christmas gift of a chemistry set from your grandparents that ignited my passion for science, technology and the world of opportunities they could address. Unbeknownst to me at the time, this set me on a life journey and love affair with the interface of technology, business and the pressing needs of society. Likewise, it was my childhood passion for rock 'n roll music and performing that guided me to an entrée in the entertainment world, and the subsequent professional success that followed.

So Julia, as you travel your own personal path, you may experience many different "lives" just as I have. Each may well be distinct from the other, initiated at a fork in the road, a consequence of your choice at those junctures, yet all of them will be embraced in some way by your deep personal Essence.

It's like parallel universes; there are different outcomes depending on the one you choose. Or, you may be destined to live but one or two lives, with equally intense passion, satisfaction and success, and as I have said, that can be just as incredibly rewarding as any many-lives experience.

My advice is don't let anyone—me, your mother, your friends, your teachers, the government—anyone—tell you what you must be or must do. Yes, you should listen carefully to understand various points of view, but in a moment of your own truth, only you can know which path to take. I suggest that you be as still as you can and listen to the omens.

Pay no attention to that beguiling voice inside you that will often prod your psyche with, "I really should do this, or I should be that." It will grab the seat of your soul with a strangulating grip, and never let go. That mischievous captivating voice is somehow imprinted in all of us through subtle injections of a subconscious potion of well-intended "advice and wisdom."

It's concocted and brewed early on by the often very well-intentioned counsel of parents, teachers, and friends—and of course, that monster we call the media. If you follow their advice and your heart says it just doesn't fit, the end product is almost never a happy and fulfilled you. Don't try living someone else's life; it can't be done!

As written so insightfully within the pages of Paulo Coelho's The Alchemist, "Listen to the omens of the Universe." She is a wise and fair maiden. She knows what all of us should do in the big picture to continue the evolution of Cosmic Consciousness, that positive energy and universal intelligence that somehow permeates all things, everywhere. In my view, it's the primary reason we are here. And only the universe knows what should be your destiny to optimize your contribution to creation and the continued and eternal evolution of consciousness.

But She is not pushy, and She will accept your choices, for free-will is truly alive and well. As I say Julia, the outcomes will be quite different for each of the choices at those junctures in your life. So, be wise—be present—be patient, and listen carefully—stay hungry—and work very hard. All of the omens are there. They are waiting for you to recognize and embrace them, each already written on the pages of your destiny.

I love you!
Dad

BIBLIOGRAPHY

Jim Al-Khalili, *Quantum: A Guide For The Perplexed*, Phoenix Illustrated, London, 2008.

Cleve Backster, *Primary Perception: Biocommunications With Plants, Living Foods, And Human Cells*, White Rose Millennium Press, Anza, CA, 2003.

Jim Baggott, *A Beginner's Guide to Reality*, Pegasus Books, New York, 2006.

Richard Barrett, *What My Soul Told Me: A Practical Guide to Soul Activation*, Fulfilling Books, Bath, UK, 2012.

Susan Blackmore, *Consciousness: An Introduction*, Oxford University Press, Oxford, 2004.

Deepak Chopra, *The Seven Spiritual Laws of Success*, Excel Books, San Rafael, CA, 1994.

Deepak Chopra, *How to Know God: The Soul's Journey Into The Mystery of Mysteries*, Three River Press, New York, 2000.

Deepak Chopra, *The Book of Secrets: Unlocking The Hidden Dimensions of Your Life*, Harmony Books, New York, 2004.

James A. Cusumano, *Cosmic Consciousness: A Journey to Well-being, Happiness and Success*, Fortuna Libri, Prague, 2011.

James A. Cusumano, *BALANCE: The Business-Life Connection*, SelectBooks, New York, 2013.

Eknath Easwaren, *The Bhagavad Gita*, Nilgiri Press, Berkeley, CA, 1985.

Eknath Easwaren, *The Upanishads*, Nilgiri Press, Berkeley, CA, 1987.

Neville Goddard, *The Essential Collection: Digital Edition*, 2013.

Neville Goddard, How To Manifest Your Desires, Digital Edition, 2013.

Nick Herbert, *Quantum Reality: Beyond The New Physics—An Excursion Into Metaphysics*, Anchor Books, New York, 1985.

Holger Kersten, *Jesus Lived In India: His Unknown Life Before and After the Crucifixion*, Penguin Books, New York, 1981.

Dali Lama, *Stages of Meditation*, Snow Lion Publications, Ithaca, NY, 2001.

Dali Lama, *The Art of Happiness: A Handbook for Living*, Riverhead Books, New York, 1998.

Ervin Laszlo, Stanislav Grof and Peter Russell, *The Consciousness Revolution*, Elf Rock Productions, Las Vegas, NV, 1999.

Ricardo B. Levy, *Letters To A Young Entrepreneur*, Catalytic Publishers, San Francisco, 2010.

Stefano Mancuso and Alessandra Viola, *Brilliant Green: The Surprising History and Science of Plant Intelligence*, Island Press, Washington, 2015.

Swami Prabhavananda and Christopher Isherwood, *How To Know God: The Yoga Aphorisms of Patanjali*, Vedanta Press, Hollywood, CA, 1953.

Matthieu Ricard & Trinh Xuan Thuan, *The Quantum And The Lotus: A Journey To The Frontiers Where Science And Buddhism Meet*, Three River Press, New York, 2001.

Tony Schwartz, *Be Excellent at Anything*, Free Press, New York, 2010.

Eckhart Tolle, *The Power of NOW*, Namaste Publishing, Novato, California, 1999.

Eckhart Tolle, *A New Earth*, Penguin Books, New York, 2005.

B. Alan Wallace, *The Attention Revolution: Unlocking The Power of The Focused Mind*, Wisdom Publications, Boston, 2006.

Ken Wilbur—Editor, *Quantum Questions: Mystical Writings of The World's Greatest Physicists*, Shambala, Boston, 2001.

Fred Alan Wolf, *The Spiritual Universe: How Quantum Physics Proves The Existence of The Soul*, Simon & Schuster, New York, 1996.

ENDNOTES

Acknowledgements

1   Ricardo B. Levy, *Letters To A Young Entrepreneur*, Catalytic Publishers, San Francisco, 2010.

Preface

2   http://www.brainyquote.com/quotes/quotes/r/robertbyrn101054. html?src=t_purpose.

3   http://jamescusumano.com/balance.

4   James A. Cusumano, *BALANCE: The Business-Life Connection*, Select Books, New York, 2013, chapter 1.

5   James A. Cusumano, *COSMIC CONSCIOUSNESS: A Journey to Well-being, Happiness and Success*, (in English and in Czech within the same volume), Fortuna Libri, Prague, 2011.

6   James A. Cusumano, *BALANCE: The Business-Life Connection*, Select Press, New York, 2013. Published in Czech as *ROVNOVAHA*, Fortuna Libri, Prague, 2013.ed.

7   Op. cit., references 5 and 6.

8   As noted throughout this text, Cosmic Consciousness refers to Universal Intelligence, the Divine, the Hindu Brahmin, or God; Personal Consciousness refers to the Divine within the individual, i.e., the Hindu Atman; and Collective Consciousness does not refer to anything like psychological "group-think," but instead to the connection of all Personal Consciousness, i.e., all Atman throughout the universe. Therefore, as proper nouns, these terms are capitalized throughout.

9   http://en.wikipedia.org/wiki/Spirituality.

10 I will use the traditional "Him" when I speak of God, but as we shall see, God is a Universal Intelligence which is genderless.

Chapter 1: Consciousness Is Everything

11 *Auguries of Innocence* by William Blake.

12 Op. cit., Reference 5.

13 Personal Consciousness is sometimes referred to as the Higher Self or, on occasion, Superconsciousness.

14 Sir James H. Jeans, *Physics and Philosophy*, University Press, Cambridge, England 1943.

15 Neville Goddard, *Neville Goddard: The Essential Collection.*

16 We will discuss the *Law of Assumption* in Part 2 as one off the elements in the Manifestation process.

17 Op. cit., reference 15.

18 Estimates between 40 and 100 trillion cells are reported in the literature. I believe that 40 trillion is the more accurate number for an average weight human being, e.g., 150 lbs (68 kg).

19 What is so magical, a better word might be "stellar," is that every one of these atoms, with the exception of hydrogen and helium, was created during the early age of the universe. They formed by nuclear fusion of lighter elements within the interior of stars, and subsequent to supernova explosion of these stars, seeded the universe with its 91 naturally-occurring elements so that all matter might be formed.

20 Pierre Teilhard de Chardin, *Le Phénomène Humain,* translated by Bernard Wall, Harper & Brothers, New York, 1955.

21 http://www.famousscientists.org/jagadish-chandra-bose/

22 Cleve Backster, *Primary Perception — Biocommunication with Plants, Foods, and Human Cells,* White Rose Millennium Press, Anza, California, 2003.

23 Anil Ananthaswamy, "Roots of Consciousness," *NewScientist, December 6, 2014, p. 34-37.*

24 Ibid.

25 Stefano Mancuso and Alessandra Viola, *Brilliant Green: The Surprising History and Science of Plant Intelligence,* Island Press, Washington, 2015.

26 Richard Karban, *Plant Sensing And Communication*, The University of Chicago Press, Chicago, 2015.

27 Eckhart Tolle, A New Earth, Penguin Books, New York, 2005, p. 277.

28 Omniscience refers to all-knowing, the total knowledge of the universe; omnipotent refers to all powerful; and omnipresence refers to present everywhere in the universe and beyond..

29 Alain Aspect, *CNRS News, http://www2.cnrs.fr/en/447.htm.*

30 Jacob Aron, *Quantum Weirdness Is Reality*, NewScientist, September 5, 2015, pp. 8-9.

31 See reference 28 for a contextual definition of these terms.

32 http://flavorwire.com/487357/astounding-carl-sagan-quotes-about-the-wonders-of-the-cosmos/view-all.

33 http://www.brainyquote.com/quotes/quotes/b/buddha378282.html.

34 http://www.scientificamerican.com/article/when-does-consciousness-arise/.

35 See the section entitled, *Reincarnation—Really? in Chapter 3.*

36 One of the best translations of Patanjali's Yoga Aphorisms is *How to Know God: The Yoga Aphorisms of Patanjali* by Swami Prabhavananda and Christopher Isherwood, Vedanta Press, Hollywood, California, 1952.

37 Ibid.

38 http://en.wikipedia.org/wiki/Subconscious.

39 Quoted in an interview by G.S. Viereck, October 26, 1929. Reprinted in "Glimpses of the Great" (1930).

40 *Neville Goddard: The Essential Collection; Collected Works by Neville Goddard,* Digital Edition, 2013, Location 2490.

41 Ibid.

Chapter 2: Consciousness And Reality

42 http://physics.about.com/od/nielsbohr/tp/Niels-Bohr-Quotes.htm.

43 http://en.wikipedia.org/wiki/Mind%E2%80%93body_problem.

44 https://en.wikipedia.org/wiki/Remote_viewing.

45 George William Russell, *The Candle of Vision*, The Library of Alexandria 1, 1918.

46 http://www.iop.org/news/13/mar/page_59670.html.

47 Albert Einstein and Alex Ayers, *Quotable Einstein, An A to Z Glossary of Quotations,* Actually, Einstein's quote was more accurately written in a letter

to his friend Michele Besso in March 1955 as, "People like us, who believe in physics, know that the distinction between past, present, and future is only a stubbornly persistent illusion," Quotable Wisdom Books, 2015.

48 Eugene Wigner, "Remarks on the Mind-Body Question," in *Quantum Theory and Measurement, Edited by John Archibald Wheeler and Wojciech Hubert Zurek*, Princeton Legacy Press, Princeton, New Jersey, 2014.

49 Michael Slezak, "Quantum Wave Function Gets Real," *NewScientist, February 7, 2015, p. 14.*

50 James A. Cusumano, *Cosmic Consciousness: Are We Truly Connected,* Fortuna Libra, Prague, 2011.

51 http://en.wikipedia.org/wiki/John_Archibald_Wheeler.

52 http://quantumenigma.com/nutshell/notable-quotes-on-quantum-physics/.

53 John Stewart Bell, *On the Einstein Podolsky Rosen Paradox*, Physics Vol. 1 (3), 1964, pp. 195-200.

Chapter 3: Is There More To You Than Your Physical Body?

54 http://www.goodreads.com/quotes/tag/spirit.

55 https://www.facebook.com/Thich.Nhat.Hanh.Quotes/posts/211735995572039.

56 M. R. Franks, *The Universe and Multiple Realities,* iuniverse, Inc. Publishers (www.iuniverse.com), Lincoln, NE, 2003.

57 Eckhart Tolle, The Power of Now, A Guide to Spiritual Enlightenment, Namaste Publishing, Novato, CA, 1999, p. 142.

Chapter 4: The Path To Fulfillment

58 http://www.brainyquote.com/quotes/keywords/fulfillment.html.

59 https://www.youtube.com/watch?v=nj2ofrX7jAk.

60 The Bhagavad Gita, Introduced and Translated by Eknath Easwaren, Nilgiri Press, Berkeley, California, 2007.

61 http://www.towerswatson.com/Insights/IC-Types/Survey-Research-Results/2012/07/2012-Towers-Watson-Global-Workforce-Study.

62 Arianna Huffington, Thrive: The Third Metric to Redefining Success and Creating a Life of Well-Being, Wisdom, and Wonder, Harmony Press, New York, 2015.

Chapter 5: What Is The True Nature of Our Universe?

63 Martin Reiss, Astronomer Royal and former President of the Royal Society, as quoted in *Quantum Enigma*, Oxford University Press, New York, 2008, Chapter 17.

64 A singularity for our purpose is defined as a point in space-time in which gravitational forces cause matter to have an infinite density and zero volume. Think of it as a mighty small point in the Absolute Infinite Nothingness, containing all of the energy and matter that our universe will ever have.

65 Gaia Theory asserts that living organisms and their inorganic surroundings have evolved together as a single living system that greatly affects the chemistry and conditions of Earth's surface. See http://www.gaiatheory.org/overview/.

66 *The Universe*, edited by John Brockman, chapters 2 and 6, HarperCollins, New York, 2014.

67 http://www.accesstoinsight.org/lib/authors/various/wheel186.html.

68 Anonymous, *Egyptian Book of the Dead, Papyrus of Nebseni (British Museum, No. 9,900, Sheets 23 and 24)*.

Chapter 6: What Single Fundamental Force Governs The Destiny of Our Universe?

69 http://www.goodreads.com/quotes/907658-nothing-is-impossible-for-pure-love.

70 https://www.google.cz/?gfe_rd=cr&ei=NEXOVImuA8WG8QeJ4YCoAQ&gws_rd=ssl#safe=active&q=define+love.

71 http://www.gaiatheory.org/overview/.

72 See the full prayer in Appendix A.

73 Eckhart Tolle, A New Earth, Penguin Books, New York, 2005, p. 7.

Chapter 7: Balancing Masculine-Feminine Energies

74 http://www.brainyquote.com/quotes/quotes/r/rainermari101352.html

75 http://thesecret.tv/.

76 http://www.bongiornoproductions.com/THE_RULE/THE_RULE.html.

77 NewScientist, March 28, 2015, p. 5.

78 Fred Pearce, NewScientist, March 28, 2015, p. 12.

79 NewScientist, March 28, 2015, p.5.

80 http://en.wikipedia.org/wiki/Pauline_Christianity.

81 For a detailed account of illegal and complicit intrigue by the Catholic Church over the centuries, consult *God's Bankers* by highly-recognized investigative author, Gerald Posner. Seven years in the making, the author clearly, accurately and objectively portrays intricate details of the formation and operation of the Vatican Bank and its partnerships with numerous illegal entities including the Italian mafia. Key elements of the book are summarized in a *New York Times Book Review* at http://www.nytimes.com/2015/03/22/books/review/gods-bankers-by-gerald-posner.html.

82 Eckhart Tolle, *A New Earth—Awakening To Your Life's Purpose*, Penguin Group, New York, 2005, Kindle Edition, location 1795.

83 http://energyfanatics.com/2014/09/02/balancing-divine-feminine-masculine-energy/;http://whatismetaphysics.com/masculine-energy-versus-feminine-energy/.

84 Op. cit.

85 Holger Kersten, *Jesus Lived in India: His Unknown Life Before and After the Crucifixion,* Penguin, 20th Printing Edition, December 31, 2001. This is a well researched analysis of the life of Christ.

86 Ibid. reference 82

87 Pierre Teilhard de Chardin, *The Evolution of Chastity*, 1934.

88 John Galsworthy, *The Forsyte Saga: Indian Summer of A Forsyte*, Oxford Paperbacks, 2008.

Chapter 8: The Art And Science of Meditation

89 The techniques I describe here are similar to those I present in my book *Cosmic Consciousness: A Journey to Well-being, Happiness and Success, Appendix B*, Fortuna Libri, Prague, 2011.

90 D. H. Lawrence, *The Complete Poems of D. H. Lawrence*, Wordsworth Editions Limited, 1994, p. 506.

91 http://newsoffice.mit.edu/2011/meditation-0505.

92 Matthieu Ricard, Antoine Lutz and Richard J. Davidson, "Mind of the Meditator," *Scientific American*, pp. 22-29, November 2014.

93 http://abcnews.go.com/Health/International/man-eat-drink/story?id=10787036.

94   https://books.google.cz/books?isbn=1452595763

95   Both are describe with other breathing techniques in great detail and in Western style language in *The Hindu-Yogi Science of Breath* by William Walker Atkinson.

Chapter 9: Creating Your Dreams

96   Goddard, Neville, *Prayer: The Art Of Believing.*

97   I use the word "create" here to mean that you have complete freewill to choose the outcome you desire. As discussed in Part 1, all creation is already done. We simply have the opportunity to choose from a large number of possibilities for a given desired manifestation.

98   James A. Cusumano, *Cosmic Consciousness: Are We Truly Connected,* Fortuna Libra, Prague, 2011, p. 38.

99   Neville Goddard, Neville Goddard: *The Essential Collection.*

100   http://www.technologyreview.com/view/427174/einsteins-spooky-action-at-a-distance-paradox-older-than-thought/.

101   http://discovermagazine.com/2002/jun/featuniverse.

102   Neville Goddard, *The Art of Believing.*

103   This wording adapted from a book on Inspirational Leadership by Lance Secretan, *The Spark, the Flame and the Torch: Change yourself. Change the World.* (Secretan Center Press, 2010).

104   Loredana Popasav, Transformative Coach, Making Change Work UK. www.MakingChangeWork.co.uk.

105   Deepak Chopra, *The Seven Spiritual Laws of Success: A Practical Guide to The Fulfillment of Your Dreams,* New World Library and Amber-Allen Publishing, San Rafael, California, 1994.

106   Deepak Chopra, *The Seven Spiritual Laws of Success: A Practical Guide to The Fulfillment of Your Dreams,* New World Library and Amber-Allen Publishing, San Rafael, California, 1994.

Chapter 10: Finding Lifelong Fulfillment

107   Vikki Corona, *Tahitian Choreographies* Volume 11, Book 18, P. 36, Dance Fantasy Productions, Printed by Dennis Bolton Enterprises, North Hollywood, California, 1989.

108   https://en.wikipedia.org/wiki/J._K._Rowling.

109 A few of these questions were suggested to me many years ago by my wise friend and personal counsel, Dr. Gay Hendricks. See *The Big Leap*, HarperOne, 2010.

110 Based on a story mentioned in reference 6, p.54.

111 How to create a Values-Based Life Plan is presented in great detail in reference 4.

112 A helpful book on personal energy management is, *Be Excellent at Anything*, Tony Schwartz, Free Press, New York, 2010.

Epilogue

113 http://www.goodreads.com/quotes/1816-you-may-say-i-m-a-dreamer-but-i-m-not-the.

114 http://intentblog.com/nature-god/.

115 Frequently referred to as *The Prayer to St. Francis*, and attributed to San Francesco d' Assisi, born Giovanni di Pietro di Bernardone (St. Francis of Assisi, 1181 – 1226), but more likely authored at the turn of the 20th century by a French priest, Father Esther Bouquerel, founder of *La Ligue de la Sainte-Messe*.

A Letter To Julia

116 Based on an article by the author entitled, *Listen to The Omens—A Letter to Julia*, Published in LEADERS Magazine, volume III, 2010, p.104 (see: http://www.balancethebusinesslifeconnection.com/system/files/documents/4_listen_to_the_omens.pdf.)

117 http://www.metrolyrics.com/when-im-64-lyrics-beatles.html

118 V.S. Ramachandran, Neurologist, University of California, *Science News*, January 30, 2010, p. 4.

ABOUT THE AUTHOR

James A. Cusumano (www.JamesCusumano.Com) is chairman and owner of Chateau Mcely (www.chateaumcely.cz/en/homepage), chosen in 2007 by the European Union as the only "Green" 5-star, castle hotel in Central Europe, and in 2008 by the World Travel Awards as *The World's Leading Green Hotel*. It is home to Chateau Mcely Forum™ (www.ChateauMcelyForum.Com), which offers programs that promote the principles of Inspired and Conscious Leadership, and finding your Life Purpose and Long-Term Fulfillment.

As part of the forum's efforts, Dr. Cusumano fostered the creation of Leadership For Life (www.LeadershipForLife.Cz), a program that brings international change-makers to Prague and Chateau Mcely to teach the global benefits of Conscious Leadership.

He began his career during the 1950s in the field of entertainment as a recording artist. Years later, after a PhD in physical chemistry, business studies at Stanford University and as a Foreign Fellow of Churchill College at Cambridge University, he joined Exxon as a research scientist and later became their research director for Catalytic Science & Technology.

Dr. Cusumano subsequently cofounded two public companies in Silicon Valley, Catalytica Energy Systems, Inc.—devoted to clean power generation; and Catalytica Pharmaceuticals, Inc., which manufactured drugs via environmentally-benign, low-cost, catalytic technologies. While he was chairman and CEO, Catalytica

Pharmaceuticals grew in less than 5 years, from several employees to 2,000 and became more than a $1 billion enterprise.

Subsequent to his work in Silicon Valley and before buying and renovating Chateau Mcely with his wife Inez, Dr. Cusumano returned to entertainment and founded Chateau Wally Films (www.chateauwallyfilms.biz), which produced the feature film *What Matters Most* (2001: www.imdb.com/title/tt0266041), distributed in more than 50 countries.

He is the coauthor of *Freedom from Mid-East Oil* (2007) and author of *Cosmic Consciousness - A Journey to Well-being, Happiness and Success* (2011) and *BALANCE: The Business—Life Connection* (2013).

Dr. Cusumano lives in Prague with his wife Inez and their daughter Julia.

www.ingramcontent.com/pod-product-compliance
Lightning Source LLC
LaVergne TN
LVHW011155080426
835508LV00007B/422